{DO-IT-YOURSELF}

d.i.y. BEAUTY

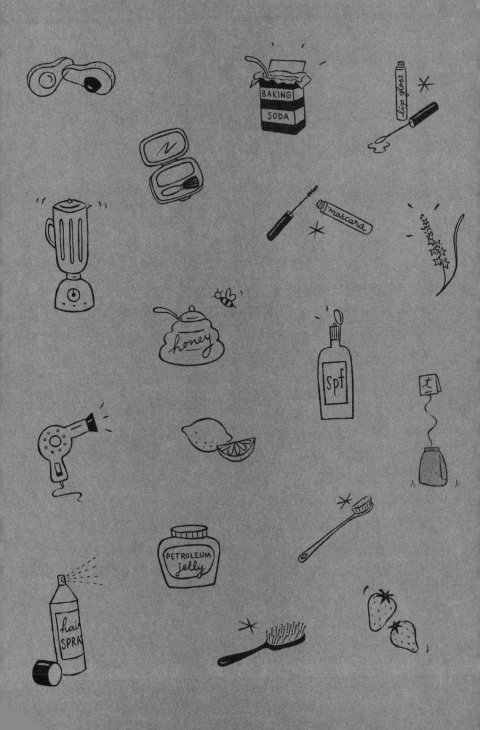

{DO-IT-YOURSELF}

d.i.y. BEAUTY

by Karen W. Bressler
& Susan Redstone

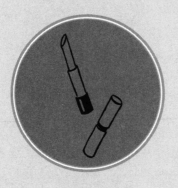

AlloyBooks

ALLOYBOOKS
Published by the Penguin Group
Penguin Putnam Books for Young Readers,
345 Hudson Street, New York, New York 10014, U.S.A.
Penguin Books Ltd, 27 Wrights Lane, London W8 5TZ, England
Penguin Books Australia Ltd, Ringwood, Victoria, Australia
Penguin Books Canada Ltd, 10 Alcorn Avenue, Toronto, Ontario, Canada M4V 3B2
Penguin Books (N.Z.) Ltd, 182-190 Wairau Road, Auckland 10, New Zealand

Penguin Books Ltd, Registered Offices: Harmondsworth, Middlesex, England

Published by Puffin Books,
a division of Penguin Putnam Books for Young Readers, 2000

1 3 5 7 9 10 8 6 4 2

Cover photo courtesy VCG/FPG International
Interior design by Lauren Monchik
Interior illustrations by Neryl Walker/Arts Council

Produced by 17th Street Productions,
an Alloy Online, Inc. company
33 West 17th Street
New York, NY 10011

ISBN 0-14-130918-0

Printed in the United States of America

THANKS TO:

Matt Diamond, Jim Johnson, and Sam Gradess
for the opportunity;
Susan Kaplow for the vision;
Jodi Anderson for the way she rules;
Angie Maximo and Alexandra Marshall for the skills;
Russell Gordon and Lauren Monchik for the look;
Neryl Walker for the art;
Everyone at 17th Street Productions
and Penguin Putnam for making it all happen;
and most of all, the Alloy.com community for the inspiration.

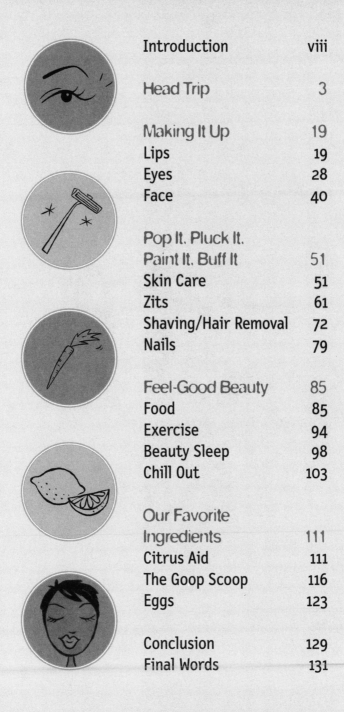

OK. like practically every girl on the planet. you care about how you look. Chances are, you're into having fewer zits and sporting a cool 'do and wearing rad makeup every once in a while. You'd probably love to find out how to get your face *really* sparkly clean and how to get your hair to stop doing that frizzy flop thing and how to make a soothing, gooey face mask.

Well, we've been reading the e-mails you've sent into Alloy.com full of a gajillion beauty tips and we can't help noticing that no one knows more about this stuff than you. And we're not talking just hair and makeup. We're talking beauty inside and out—from using a facial wash that zaps zits to experimenting with yoga to just focusing on the inner you. So here's the deal. We've put all your tips in this one book and paired them with expert advice from some of the country's top makeup artists and dermatologists. We've also added some of our own favorite recipes. And to top it all off, we've sprinkled celeb interviews, funny beauty horror stories, and funky beauty facts throughout. Best of all, we've kept it completely DIY—meaning cheap, easy, and do-it-yourself. Lots of the tips you'll see in here call for ingredients you can find in the fridge or lying around the house.

Here's a beauty book that won't insult your intelligence or blow your budget. So set aside some private time—or round up your friends—for a night of total beauty. Ready?

A NOTE FROM KAREN AND SUSAN: According to dermatologist Howard Sobel, these recipes may be effective for some, but if you have a tendency toward acne or oily skin, you should avoid the mixtures that contain oils. Also, if you have skin that gets irritated easily, steer clear of acidic ingredients like oranges, lemons, or vinegar. If you have an allergic history, make sure to look at all the ingredients first. If you have any concerns you might want to consult a dermatologist before trying these tips.

HEADTRIP

{*HAIR HELP TO FIX THOSE FOLLICLES*}

Straight, curly, short, or long, just about everyone's into their hair. Seriously . . . messing with your tresses is the most fun a girl can have from the neck up. So read on for some fantastic hairdos (and more than a few hair don'ts).

from: BECKY

In the summer and spring my friend and I always make this hair mask to make our hair soft and shiny! We got compliments on our hair the first time we used it. Ever since, it's been a tradition. You put chicken fat, oatmeal, avocado, sesame oil, coconut milk, and honey into a bowl in equal proportions. Dip in a comb and apply an even coat through your hair. After about 20 minutes, rinse. If you have light brown to blond hair, put lemon juice in as well. It makes your hair lighter.

"Natural ingredients like avocado, oatmeal, and coconut milk are used in a lot of hair and beauty products, and they will do your hair good," says Stewart Long, head of product development at Charles Worthington Hair in London. "But chicken fat is a different story. It's likely to clog the pores of the scalp and the hair follicles. Modify the recipe by cutting out the chicken fat

and using just avocado, coconut milk, and oatmeal. Your hair will get a boost of protein, extra moisture, shine, and body."

from: VALERIE

I've got some great advice for all you girls out there who love to hang out in the sun but hate the fried look it can give to your hair. All you have to do is fill a plastic spray bottle with one cup of water, one tablespoon of your favorite sunscreen (SPF 15 or higher), and one tablespoon of your favorite gel or leave-in conditioner. Then shake it up really well and stash it in your beach tote. Spray it in your hair before and during your time in the sun to keep your hair from becoming scorched by the rays. The conditioner will keep your hair soft, and the gel will keep your style in place. Your hair will thank you.

"The sunscreen idea is good," says hair color expert Leslie Louise of the Miwa-Alex Salon in New York, "but don't use hair gel in the sun. It contains alcohol, which is drying, and the sun makes this worse. You can also coat your hair in conditioner and braid it, which is a very cute style. The heat from the sun will open up the hair cuticles so the conditioner will penetrate and make the hair softer."

from: RICKY

This is a tip for my black sistas out there whose hair does

that frizzy curl-up-in-the-heat thing in the summer. At night wash your hair and then towel dry it until it's just slightly damp. Add a leave-in conditioner like Bone Strait, and then add a soft styling gel like Jam and light hair cream like Pink Lotion. Then pull it back in a bun and wrap it in a silk scarf. While you sleep, your hair will be conditioned, moisturized, and dried in a healthy fashion as opposed to blow drying it, which can break and weaken hair. In the morning, when you unwrap your hair, it should look wavy and sleek—a sexy summer look.

"If your hair is curly, this would be a good approach, but you could totally skip the overnight stuff and wash your hair in the morning, use a leave-in conditioner afterward, apply a little gel, and let it air dry," says Peter West, owner and stylist at Follicles Hair Spa in Brooklyn, New York. "Don't do this with relaxed hair, though, unless you plan to style it afterward (instead of just leaving it to air dry)."

from: CAROLINE
To get silky hair, apply olive oil to your hair once a week and leave it in for about five minutes. Make sure to rinse

thoroughly, though, or the excessive oil may weigh down your hair.

"Olive oil has been used for thousands of years to soften hair," says New York stylist and salon owner Oscar Bond. "The molecular structure of olive oil doesn't really get into the actual hair shaft as well as some of the products formulated by hair companies, but try warming the olive oil first to create a hot oil treatment that will better penetrate your hair."

from: LIZ
Put baby powder in your hair to absorb the greasies!

"If your hair is a mess and you don't have time to wash it, baby powder is an okay alternative," says Coco Santiago, hairstylist at Bumble and Bumble salon in New York. "The powder will get rid of some of the greasies as it coats the hair, absorbs oil, and adds tons of volume. But only use it if you're blond because the white will make other hair colors look chalky. And don't use talc—it's too heavy."

from: JUSTINE
About once a month I mix together half a cup of mayo, half a cup of vegetable oil, two eggs, and a quarter cup of my

regular conditioner (the conditioner is just to add a nice smell). I then put my creation (as I call it) in my hair and leave it for about an hour. Then I jump in the shower and shampoo and condition my hair normally. This makes my hair shiny, smooth, and soft.

"Mayo is great for hair—so if you haven't tried it yet, you should," says New York spa owner and Chinese beauty expert Helen Lee. "However, this concoction is a bit too much. Mayo already contains eggs and oil, so you don't need to add either of these things to the mixture."

from: LEAH
Ever get dry, frizzed-out hair after blow drying? Here's a tip: Use cool air—it'll take a little longer, but it's worth it!

Yep—it certainly is worth it. "The cool air protects the hair shaft and locks in moisture, giving it more sheen and less of the frizzies," says Nelson Vercher, a stylist at Oribe Salon in New York. "If you blow-dry your hair every day, a cool setting is the way to go, especially if your hair is already damaged."

from: LULU
For really shiny hair I rinse out my conditioner with warm water. I then rinse quickly with cool water and wrap my hair in a towel. It really works!

Just like blow drying with cool air, a cold rinse is great for your hair. "The warm water is great for this," says hairstylist Nelson Vercher, "as it enables conditioner to penetrate the hair shaft. When you follow with a cool rinse, it locks in the moisture."

from: CHELSEA

Dip a clean mascara wand into hair gel, then run it through your hair where you have cowlicks. It'll really get those stray strands to stay where you want!

"Yeah, this is a really good idea! You can also use a fine-tooth comb or, to control bigger sections, you can even use your hairbrush," says New York–based hairstylist Steven Shames.

from: BETH

A great one: I use Jell-O for gel. That's right! I have that funky, spiked hair look, and I make it all possible with ready-to-eat Jell-O.

Stylist Steven Shames agrees. "Jell-O contains gelatin, which is protein made from cows' hooves. And protein is great conditioning for your hair."

from: RAINBOW99

If you have brittle hair, apply conditioner to damp hair and wrap in a hot towel for thirty minutes. Then rinse.

"This is a good idea," says stylist Steve Berg, "but my favorite trick in the book is to put conditioner on dry hair once a week and let it soak in for fifteen minutes before washing as normal." The dry hair trick works because wet hair is already saturated with water; dry hair can better absorb the conditioner.

I was curling my hair getting ready for school one day, and I was late so my mom came in to get me. Surprised, I spun my head and SMACK!—the curling iron went straight into my neck! My mom wouldn't let me stay home so I had to go to school like that. Everyone at school was asking me if I had a HICKEY on my neck. I was so embarrassed!

—STRAWBERRY

from: KEA

After your styling is done, stick your hair in front of a fan for a minute or two. The look you're aiming for is carefree and fun, and the fan will make straightened hair look supersexy.

"This is a great idea for straight hair," agrees hairstylist Nelson Vercher. "But don't stand there too long, or it will start to tangle!" Depending on how wild you want to get, this could also work for wavy hair, but beware of blowing really curly hair into a giant fuzz ball!

from: JACKIE

You may have heard that you shouldn't start blow drying your hair till it's 75 percent dry, but it won't matter if you do. In fact, you should start blow drying it sooner so you don't allow any frizzies to develop.

"If you have straight hair, you can wait to blow-dry it until it's almost dry naturally and not have to worry about frizzies," says hairstylist Nelson Vercher. "But if you have curly hair, you need to tackle the job right away. That way the water will weigh it down, the moisture will be locked in, and frizzies will have less of a chance to start."

from: BUFFSTER

If your hair feels heavy from too many hair products or chlorine, then try using baking soda and warm water to get it feeling clean.

"This does work," say colorist Doug MacIntosh of the Minardi Salon in New York. "Baking soda acts as a light but abrasive cleanser on your hair (so don't overdo it). For the best effect, add some to your shampoo."

from: CLARISSA

If you have layers, blow-dry your hair with your head down and your hair flipped over. This gives it more body.

"Yes, it does," says celebrity hairdresser Charles Worthington, who's styled the coifs of many stars including Kate Winslet. "But be careful not to completely dry the hair, or you could end up looking like a scarecrow. Rough dry it while fluffing with your hands to get a 'root lift,' but stop while it's still damp enough to style at the ends."

from: PONCHOLAYDEE

You know those frizzies at the top of your head that tend to stick out? What I do is rub some type of lotion on my hands and then run my fingers through my hair (don't overdo it or it will look superoily), and then I brush my hair. It works—try it.

"For flyaway strands on the top of the head, a dab of skin moisturizer on your hands is a good way to flatten them

down," says stylist Oscar Bond. "Be sure to just use a teeny-weeny bit, and don't bother running your hands through your whole head of hair since there's no benefit to coating it under-neath."

from: DIANE

To get a bump-free ponytail, follow these steps:

1. Lay across your bed with you hair hanging off the bed

2. Brush out your hair (be careful if you have bangs not to brush them up too!)

3. Pull your hair into a ponytail and secure with a pony-tail holder

4. If you want, brush out your ponytail. Ta da! your ponytail is complete!

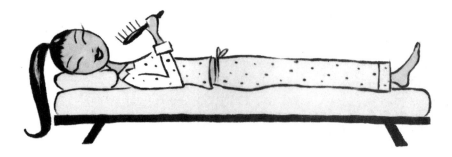

"Yes, this will work if you want a really tight ponytail fixed on the top of your head," says stylist Nikki Padula of the Minardi Salon in New York. "Another way to get a totally bump-free ponytail is to pull it all back and secure it really loosely with a scrunchie, which won't leave a dent in the hair."

from: SUSANNA

If your hair is frizzy, just apply clear mascara to that disaster hair ball!!!

"You should probably think twice about this one," says celebrity hairdresser Charles Worthington. "If you have a clear mascara that doesn't set completely hard, then it's fine for brushing those temperamental hairs away from the hairline. However, beware of mascara that sets rock hard—you don't want to end up with a head that looks like crispy bacon."

from: SOMETHING

During the weekends or whenever you're not going to school, don't blow-dry or curl your hair. The hot air from the blow-dryer can damage it, so when you can, give your hair some time off.

"Good idea," says Stewart Long of Charles Worthington Hair. "Even though hair products have come a long way, heat and styling will damage the hair, and it's very hard to correct that. The best prevention is to use a heat-and-damage protector, but other than that, the less you heat style it, the better."

from: SWEETLADY
Mix half a cup of cranberry juice and water and pour on your hair to get rid of chlorine.

"Chlorine is a notoriously hard chemical to get out of hair, and you need a strong ingredient to get it out," says Stewart Long. "The best thing is a shampoo designed just for that. There's no proof that a rinse of cranberry juice will dechlorinate your hair, but it will do some good; it's crammed full of antioxidants that protect hair from things like the sun. Be careful to use a very dilute solution, and don't do it too often since the fruit acid will be too harsh if used over and over."

One time I used an at-home kit and dyed my hair "midnight black" for the school musical. It was supposed to be semipermanent, but as the months went by, it didn't wash out at all! It was still really black by the time summer rolled around, and my head used to get so hot that I couldn't sit next to a window without a hat on!

—SAMMY

MELISSA AUF DE MAUR

The red-hot bassist for Smashing Pumpkins (and formerly Hole) shares her theories on role models and red hair. . . .

How did you feel about your looks when you were younger?

Growing up with curly red hair and freckles, I always knew one thing for sure: I wasn't like everyone else. Luckily I've never suffered from extreme self-hate, but when I was a kid, my motto was, Maybe if I'm really quiet, I'll disappear. So I just hoped people wouldn't notice that I looked different; I did not want to stick out. Once I grew out of the teenage dilemma of wanting to be the same as others and grew into the individual who is me, Melissa, I became (and remain) proud of my curly red hair and freckles! I am different, and I am proud.

Whether it's because we're derived from aliens or we're some extinct breed or we're freaks of nature (these are, of course, some of the theories about us redheads), I truly believe there's a secret bond among all redheads throughout the world and the ages. I notice and salute every one of us when I see one.

Did you ever try to cover up your freckles?

Covering up freckles is an impossible task. I just stayed out of the sun so I wouldn't get more.

What about dealing with your hair?

The longer curly hair gets, the straighter it gets, so I obsessively grew my hair. But as I learned, every head of hair has a limit to how long it can grow, and mine will never grow longer than my upper back. I'd cry every time I got a trim (I still do!), and I never got to have down-to-the-bum mermaid hair. Well, except for now, with extensions for photo shoots—the secret fun of fulfilling your hair fantasies for a day . . .

What was your style in high school?

Having curly hair, I didn't have a lot of hairstyle options except for cutting it short or wearing it long. When it's long, you can wear it in a braid, and you get the illusion of having straight hair. But when it's short, you're in Afro land. For one brief New Wave period in my teens, I had short hair, parted on the side and coming down over one of my eyes. I'd never do that again. No, no, no.

Above all else, I was shy. I wore no makeup (anything not to stand out). The misfit in me (you know, red hair, believes in ghosts and astrology . . .) made me feel isolated and depressed, so I dressed in lots of boy-style army surplus clothes: combat boots, long johns, green dickeys, army green sweaters. At least the green went with my hair and green eyes, but it wasn't intentional.

Who is your biggest beauty role model?

My mother is the most beautiful woman in the world to me.

We're polar opposites: She's dark and exotic, with high cheekbones, full lips, and olive skin. Everyone thought I was adopted. I'm in awe of her beauty, but then she also loves me more than anyone, and unconditional love always equals beauty.

If you had to pull something out of your refrigerator and use it as a beauty product, what would it be?

Lemon to clean with and olive oil to moisturize. When I'm not on the road, I use various beauty products, but I like them mild and minimal.

When in your life have you felt the most beautiful?

I was quite a tomboy growing up, so I felt sort of pretty but like a young boy is pretty (I was a late bloomer, too. I was skinny and had no curves anywhere). I never felt ugly; I just thought I looked like a boy. It wasn't until I became a woman (around the age of twenty-five) that I ever felt beautiful. Becoming a woman involves many things, like getting more curves on your body, more definition in your face, loss of baby fat ... but most of all, you grow on the emotional, mental, and experience levels. It's funny—once you feel like a woman on the inside, you look like one on the outside, and everyone knows that all women are beautiful.

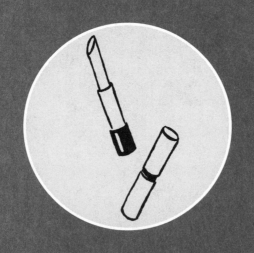

MAKING IT UP

TRICKS AND TIPS FOR MAKING MAKEUP EASY TO DO

So it's not rocket science. But who hasn't worn the wrong color lipstick or gone too heavy on the eyeliner? Drawing the perfect pout or applying your blush just right isn't exactly easy. Need some schooling? Okay, let's go back to the basics. . . .

•LIPS•

from: SHANI

When you want to blot your lipstick, don't blot with a tissue because you'll get yucky stuff on your lips. Blot with a coffee filter as many times as you like and then trash it. You won't have any gunk on your lips, and you'll be totally satisfied.

> *"The reason why tissue gets stuck on your lips is because it's made of wood fibers, but a coffee filter is composed of concentrated pressed paper," says makeup artist Jim Crawford of Garren New York Salon. "You can even cut the coffee filter into squares and stockpile it in your bathroom so you're always prepared."*

from: ELLA D.

After applying a gloss or lipstick, dab a bit of white eye shadow in the center of your lower lip and rub your lips together until it looks subtle. It gives your mouth that full, sexy, pouty look.

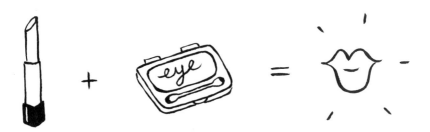

"Great tip," says makeup artist Laura Geller of Laura Geller Makeup Studios in New York, "but put on a shimmery white shadow instead of a matte color to get a poutier effect—the shimmer will give the lower lip even more dimension."

from: HONEYCOMB '84

If you want your lip color to be dazzling without your lip gloss applicator getting all lipsticky, then put your lip color on your bottom lip and gloss on the upper one and rub them together.

"This is not a good idea," says Lindsay Ebbin, a makeup artist at Elizabeth Arden salons. "You'll get an uneven lip line plus smudges and color bleeding from the edges, too. Instead apply your lip liner first all

the way around, fill in with lip liner, and apply lipstick on top. Then take a dab of gloss on your baby finger and rub over the bottom lip and blot really quickly. This way your lip gloss applicator won't get sticky."

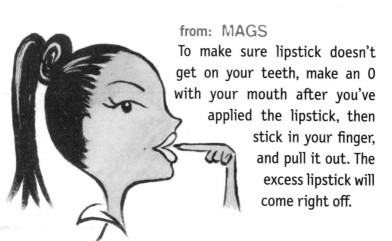

lipliner

from: COURTNEY

Instead of wasting the last of your lipstick by throwing it away, get an old ice tray and cut bits of lipstick into the square compartments. Then mix with lip gloss colors.

"This is a good recycling idea," says makeup artist Ramy Gafni. "You could also go to any drugstore and pick up a plastic pillbox very cheaply to put your scraps of lip gloss in. You can use a cotton swab to scoop out the old lipstick, and you don't need to add gloss, either—you can use it straight. It's best applied with a lip brush."

from: MAGS

To make sure lipstick doesn't get on your teeth, make an 0 with your mouth after you've applied the lipstick, then stick in your finger, and pull it out. The excess lipstick will come right off.

"There is no better way to do this, and it really does work!"
says Ramy Gafni. "Just make sure your fingers are clean!"

from: WEETZIE1
Rub an ice cube on your lips after applying lipstick to lock in your color.

"This isn't going to work," says makeup artist Lindsay Ebbin. "Ice is water, and the same thing will happen as when you drink a glass of water—your lipstick will come off. The best way to get lipstick to stay is to follow these steps:

1. Apply foundation to lips

2. Powder to set

3. Apply lipstick and gloss

4. Blot with tissue

For all-day wear use a lip pencil underneath your lipstick. This will guarantee that a base tone shows through anytime the topcoat wears off.

from: SABRINA
One way to make your lips look fuller is to dab a concealer that's lighter than your foundation color onto your bottom lip. You have to dab it from corner to corner, then

blend it until only you can see it. It works well, I promise.

"Use a foundation or concealer that tends to be opaque and is one shade lighter than your regular foundation," suggests makeup artist Jim Crawford. "Apply a dab to the center of both the bottom and the top lip, using your fingertip or a cotton swab. Blend until you can't see the line of demarcation, then apply lipstick to create fuller-looking lips."

from: DARYL

I have a great beauty tip that makes your puckers totally watchable! First you find a lip line color that you really love and put it on all across your bottom lip and most of the top lip. Then you put on some clear or clearish pink gloss, and voilà, a totally cute color with a little liner!

Good idea! Makeup artist Laura Geller also has this tip: "Use lip balm or vitamin E lipstick all over your mouth. Dip a lip brush into your favorite pearlized eye shadow, either a pink, silver, or white frost; paint on top of the Chap Stick; then smack your lips together. Add a little more vitamin E or clear gloss on top, and you get a shiny, great-looking mouth."

LIPSTICK TRACES

Max Factor, 1958: "A woman who doesn't wear lipstick feels undressed in public. Unless she works on a farm."

1950s

World War II has ended, and women are ready for a little glamour.

1952: Revlon's Fire & Ice campaign is the first real lipstick media blitz.

1957: Gala introduces Lipline, the first lipstick in a tube, abolishing time-consuming brush-on application.

1959: Tony Curtis and Jack Lemmon pucker up and paint it on for *Some Like It Hot.*

1960s

Women start to break out of traditional roles and break old-hat beauty rules.

1960: To prove she's not a prostitute, Elizabeth Taylor's *Butterfield 8* party girl writes No Sale on a man's mirror in blush pink lipstick (before walking out in his wife's mink).

1964: Dusty Springfield releases "I Only Want to Be with You," and white lipstick truly becomes the next big thing.

1966: Catering to mod

24

princesses everywhere, Mary Quant launches the first makeup artist line and declares heavy lipstick "out" and pale gloss "in"; gloss aficionado Twiggy declared Face of the Year by Britain's *Daily Express*.

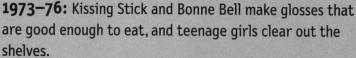

After the naturalism of the 1960s and the gains of women's lib, people are ready to get wild with their looks.

1972: Women's libbers take off their lipstick while David Bowie puts it on.

1973–76: Kissing Stick and Bonne Bell make glosses that are good enough to eat, and teenage girls clear out the shelves.

1977: Punk rockers hit the pinnacle of antichic with basic black while disco divas party down in Yves Saint Laurent's new fuschia gloss.

Reagan reigns. But here and there, fashion rebels thrive.

1982: The crooked lip line is vindicated when Robert Smith and The Cure hit it big with "Let's Go to Bed."

1984: Wham's "Wake Me Up Before You Go Go" video (unfortunately) launches the fluorescent lipstick trend. David Bowie's video for "China Girl" reminds us that sometimes a bright red mouth looks better messed up.

1986: It's a red-letter day for flawless lips with Robert Palmer's none-too-feminist "Addicted to Love" video.

Madonna declares M•A•C's Russian Red her favorite color, and stores can't keep it in stock.

1987: The members of Poison glam it up, signaling that subtle lip gloss even rocks on heavy metal boys.

Lipstick becomes a vehicle for activism, but scores of women still can't get liner stains off their cell phones!

1994: M•A•C puts lipstick to work for humanity by launching the new shade Viva Glam and donating all the proceeds to AIDS charities.

1996–present: Lip stains make a natural-looking mouth more popular than perfect red lips; nontransfer lipsticks make it safe to smooch without fear of rubbing off; the success of random lipstick options like blue and glitter prove that finally, where your lips are concerned, anything goes.

1998: Marilyn Manson releases the glam CD "Mechanical Animals" and his main squeeze Rose McGowan admits they share lipsticks; Marilyn hasn't been seen without at least some lip liner since.

1999: The biggest impact of Monica Lewinsky's Barbara Walters appearance is that Club Monaco can't keep the lip gloss Monica wore (Glaze) for the interview on the shelves.

1990s

At the outset of the new millennium women experiment with their looks like never before, but Gwyneth, Julia, and Sarah Jessica still look prettiest in pink; cyberheroines like Tomb Raider's Lara Croft make digital desirable.

2000: Aromatherapy glosses like Bloom's Lip Glaze throw a little dharma into the disco. French department store Sephora opens its massive Rockefeller Center store in New York, filled to bursting with more shades of green lipstick than anyone ever thought possible. Bright orange gloss hits the stores for spring, giving new meaning to juicy lips.

2001: With yummy lipstick all the rage, will Matte Meatloaf be the next hot (and savory) seller?

2003: With plastic surgery getting less unusual—but more expensive—cherry-flavored wax lips may be making a comeback.

2008: Madonna is still fabulous at the ripe old age of fifty, and Lourdes turns twelve. In all likelihood, she and her mother will already be butting heads, causing M•A•C to cook up a Seeing Red stain for the occasion.

In Roman times, black kohl was used as mascara, eyebrow darkener, and eyeliner.

I decided to curl my eyelashes before this party I was going to. I sprayed a little hairspray on the eyelash curler first to make the lashes stick up the way I wanted them to. Well, they did stick—to the eyelash curler! I ended up pulling out, like, six of my eyelashes!

—ELKIE

•EYES•

from: COREY

Put hair spray on an old toothbrush to keep your eyebrows in check.

"That's a great idea," says makeup artist Ramy Gafni. "Hair gel, used in the same way, will also keep wayward brows in place."

from: KORNUT

You can get rid of close-to-the-eye smudges of mascara or eye shadow by taking a wet cotton swab and rolling it gently along your lid. It works!

"You really shouldn't do this," says makeup artist Lindsay Ebbin. "Water may smudge the color even more. The swab is the perfectly designed tool for the job, but you really need to use it with eye-makeup remover. Just be sure to use one with minimal mineral oil (check the ingredients) to prevent blocking pores around the eye."

from: NATASHA

Before using eyelash curlers, heat them with a blow-dryer to get a better-held curl.

"This is an old model's trick that's been around forever and ever," says makeup artist Laura Geller. "Heating the strip of an eyelash curler will give you a better curl that will probably last a lot longer, just as curling your hair with a warm curling iron will give your curls more staying power. Just don't let the eyelash curler get so hot that it burns your lashes and/or your eye."

I was in a musical at school, and like everyone knows, you have to put on a ton of makeup so you don't look washed out onstage. So anyway, I was complaining about my eyebrows and how they were all screwed up, so this girl offered to fill them in for me. Only she accidentally filled them in with blue pencil instead of black and didn't bother to mention her little mistake. Everyone was like, "What is up with your eyebrows?"

—THEA

from: MANDY

Try lip gloss on your eyelids. They'll shine and look really pretty. On your eyebrows use shadows like pink, baby blue, and silver—it looks pretty cool.

"Actually, lip gloss is too sticky to use on the eyes. Believe me, I've tried it," says Sandy Mustion, cocreator of Alchemy Makeup. "You won't be able to blink! If you really want that glossy look, mix powdered eye shadow with petroleum jelly (you'll still be able to blink). As far as powder in your brows? Add shimmer dust to ordinary eyebrow powder, which will look soft and pretty and enhance the brow bone and face structure. But blues and pinks may look a little weird."

from: JENNY

Hey, using old mascara brushes as brow brushes works great after you clean them.

"Make sure the brush is thoroughly cleaned and sanitized beforehand—hot water and soap will get the mascara off," says Leslie Blodgett, president of Bare Escentuals. "Dip the brush in alcohol and let it dry, then use as a brow brush."

from: RED

Before I put on mascara, I always brush a white, shimmery eye shadow underneath my bottom lash line and in the corners of my eyes. I think it makes my eyes "pop," and it gives me a fresh, clean look.

"This is true if you have beautiful skin," says Marta Sienkiewicz of Allure Day Spa and Hair Design in New York. "If you have good, evenly colored skin, try bright whites. If you have red skin, try lighter, softer whites, and first apply make-up to cover the red spots around the eyes so you have a clean color as a base."

from: CONNIE

To get rid of those icky bags under my eyes, I use hot tea bags. It kind of hurts at first, but it works so well, even better than cucumbers. Also, once the tea bag is cooled off, I usually rub it around the rest of my face because it gives me a healthy glow and makes my skin baby soft.

"Try green tea, which acts as an antioxidant, or chamomile, which is soothing and calming for sensitive skin," says Celeste Induddi, co-owner of Prema Nolita makeup shop in New York. And be sure to let those tea bags cool a little before you put them on your eyelids.

from: MAXIE

To help bags under your eyes look less puffy, just put an ice cube on 'em for about ten seconds.

Right on. "Ice cubes have long been used on the eyes to combat allergic reactions," adds Celeste Induddi.

from: DYLAN

I have the best makeup tip. Close your eyes and splash them with water before applying the mascara. The moisture on your eyelashes will keep your mascara from clumping.

"Any kind of moisture will help reduce clumps, but you might want to try wetting your lashes with clear brow gel instead since water can make your mascara run," suggests makeup artist Laura Geller. "Or try a lash conditioner."

from: ROSIE

Did you know that if you mix water and eye shadow and then put it on, it lasts all day?

"It's true that this will make it last longer. But you also need to be sure not to put a lot of moisturizer under the color," says New York makeup artist Marina Buka. "The emollients in most moisturizers can cause the color to crack."

from: AMBER

If you're going to pluck your eyebrows, here's a quick way to see which hairs need to be plucked. Take hair pomade and put it on your fingers. Wipe across brows and shape them the way you want. It will then be obvious which hairs are out of line and need to be plucked! After you do the dreaded deed, use alcohol or hydrogen peroxide on the plucked area to keep away infection and finish with a moisturizer or an aloe vera lotion to soothe.

"Many people break out from using hair-styling products on their skin, so be careful," warns Lana Bargraser, co-owner of Allure Day Spa and Hair Design in New York. "As far as cleansing the area afterward, hydrocortisone or an antiseptic product like Sea Breeze will work, too, and help heal redness at the same time. Use an antiseptic moisturizer when you're finished for extra protection."

My sister hates it when I use her makeup. But I get bored with mine, so I always sneak into her makeup bag when she's not around —her superexpensive mascara is killer. One morning she warned me not to use it 'cause she was getting a case of pinkeye. Well, I just figured she was lying to trick me, so I went ahead and used it, anyway. When I got pinkeye a couple of days later, she couldn't stop gloating.

—SOULSISTER

I used to wear black eyeliner, and like a dummy, I thought it was supposed to be put on superthick. It made me look like I hadn't slept in ten years! Total vampire eyes. When I started this "beauty trick," I noticed that all of my friends wouldn't want to be seen with me. I had no clue why. Then one day I wrote a note to this guy, asking him out. He wrote back, "As long as you don't have fangs."

—GOSHGIRL

from: POKÉWOMAN

Instead of using eye liner, you should apply a dark powder at the rim of the eyelid. It gives a more natural look that's not so dense and dark.

"You can use eye shadow this way, but apply it with a flat-angled brush," advises makeup artist Kristin Penta, creator of Fun Cosmetics. "Shake excess powder off the brush before applying it to prevent extra makeup particles from shaking onto your face and sticking there."

from: GREER

If you want smoky eyes, apply a soft brown shadow (with a fine makeup brush) to the lower lash line and use the same color on your upper lid. Then add a lighter shade over the brown shadow and partially blend it for a natural look.

For a more dramatic effect, try this tip from makeup artist Marina Buka: "Line your upper lids with dark eyeliner, then dip an eye shadow brush into a tiny bit of shadow (don't use too much, or it will flake off on your foundation) and follow the line of your lashes, blending upward without going above the crease. Blend the area closest to the crease with a lighter shade of brown. Follow the same format below the eye, applying a pencil liner to the rim of the lid and blending well. Use foundation two shades lighter than your skin tone around the brow."

GLAM GURUS

They snuck makeup into school in their backpacks and dyed their hair every color of the rainbow to create their own beauty concoctions. These beauty entrepreneurs were born to blend, highlight, and gloss.

BOBBI BROWN
BOBBI BROWN ESSENTIALS

Philosophy: Makeup for teenage girls should be fun and fresh and young, with lots of pastel shades. When you're young, you have the flexibility to wear less makeup, and less is more.

First entrepreneurial experience: "I locked myself in the bathroom at age seven and put my mother's makeup all over myself and all over the walls. As I got older, I practiced my makeup skills on my family, including my brothers!"

Advice: If you have a passion, don't ever lose sight of that dream.

WENDE ZOMNIR
URBAN DECAY

Philosophy: Be creative at home and take risks with makeup—break beauty boundaries and have fun doing it.

Earliest entrepreneurial experience: "I used to drive my mother crazy—I was always making something as a child—either little boxes or little pictures with frames. I would make lipsticks by mashing two colors together in a little jar. I even made a swimsuit once. I really enjoyed making something from nothing, and it was always important to me that people really liked what I had created. I've also always loved color,

which is what attracted me to cosmetics."

Advice: "If you want to change your look regularly, beauty products are the way to achieve it."

TONY AND TINA BORNSTEIN
TONY & TINA VIBRATIONAL REMEDIES

Philosophy: You can adjust cosmetics to suit your mood by using color energy to balance each of your individual chakra systems.

First entrepreneurial experience: "I was truly more of a tomboy as a child," says Tina. "I hung out with the boys or went off by myself, but I always had a passion for collecting colored stones, so I guess I was into color at an early age. Tony, on the other hand, started painting at around age seven, so he was always creative."

Advice: "I think that if you want to do something creative, day-dreaming is really good. It's actually a form of visualization, and usually a lot of thought goes in to it. So daydream lots, and don't shut those dreams out because you never know where they're going to lead. Once you find your vision, keep hold of it and don't get distracted!"

TISH AND SNOOKIE BELLOMO
MANIC PANIC NYC INC.

Philosophy: It's all about wigs, cosmetics, wild hair colors, and nail polish.

Earliest entrepreneurial experience: "We started with $200 each," says Snookie, "and it took a long time. We had our first punk rock boutique in New York's East Village on

St. Mark's Place back before we went solely into wholesale. At one time I was a backup singer for Blondie. I would take a rug and loom everywhere and weave backstage at gigs!"

Advice: "Don't believe people who tell you it can't or won't happen. It can. Be determined and love what you sell and sell what you love!"

LESLIE BLODGETT
BARE ESCENTUALS

Philosophy: "To bring natural formulas to people interested in improving their skin and their well-being. We use essential oils and botanical extracts from around the world to make formulas that give you a captivating experience from the moment you touch them."

Earliest entrepreneurial experience: "I was the girl who would put makeup on her dolls. In college my friends and I would get together to do masks and group facials. I would read their tarot cards and tell their futures, which would include what colors would look best on them."

Advice: "If you have passion, if you know you love makeup, if you've been playing with it for years, testing it on your hand

in the department stores and trying out all the new shades, you're halfway there. It takes someone with passion and enthusiasm to create the next new thing."

SHIRLEY MANSON'S TOP-FIVE BEAUTY SECRETS

The Rock Goddess from Garbage Lists Her Top-Five Beauty Musts

1. The secret of a beautifully made-up face is blending!!! Save your money and invest in great brushes from a good brand. Believe me ... they make the task of application so much easier.

2. Use a good-quality, finely ground face scrub at least twice a week. It will improve the look and feel of your skin.

3. Always moisturize your face first thing in the morning and last thing at night.

4. Don't ever spend a fortune on expensive nail polishes. They chip as fast—if not faster—than the cheapies.

5. You'll look better if you feel better. Figure out what works for you in this regard— whether it's drinking lots of water, getting plenty of exercise and maintaining a healthy diet, or eating snacks while sitting in front of the TV. Whatever makes you happy. That's all that matters.

· FACE·

from: JANE

I have a tip for you guys: To get a healthy glow or subtle shine on your face, use some shine-enhancing hair gloss (make sure it's oil-free) or oil-free moisturizer.

"Hair gloss isn't the best for this," says makeup artist Ramy Gafni. "These sprays for hair usually contain silicone, which can be excessively drying and block the pores on your face. You're right about the moisturizer, though. Use a lightweight reflecting moisturizer with a subtle shimmer."

from: SK8HONEY

Before you apply foundation, put lots of lotion on your skin so the foundation goes on smoother. You can also use the same lotion in your hair to make it look healthier.

"Moisturizer smooths out the skin and makes foundation much, much easier to blend in," says makeup artist Ramy Gafni. "And now they have tinted moisturizers that do both at the same time—which is really great if you don't want or need heavy coverage. As for putting lotion on your hair, many stylists recommend it, and there really are no problems with it. But I would go easy on the moisturizer, and I wouldn't use a heavy body lotion."

from: NIKKI D.

For longer-lasting makeup:

1. Put just a dab of foundation on your skin and blend all over your face (lips and eyelids included).

2. Add a tiny bit of powder on the T zone (your forehead, nose, and chin).

3. Put Vaseline on lips.

4. Put on all eye makeup (mascara/shadow/liner).

"I would try these products in this order instead," says make-up artist Ramy Gafni:

1. Apply concealer and foundation, then set with loose powder (just a tiny bit on the T zone).

2. Apply eye makeup and blush and use a nude pencil color on lips, then blot lips with tissue.

3. Lightly dust another tiny bit of loose powder everywhere, then add a coat of lipstick.

from: PURPLE_PEONY

Put a line of lipstick on each cheek and blend for a one-of-a-kind color blush that lasts all night. (Bonus—it will match your lipstick perfectly.)

"If your skin is sensitive, it isn't a good idea to put lip products on your skin—you might get a rash or break out from the bacteria that touched your mouth," says Kristin Penta, creator of FUN Cosmetics. "But if you don't have sensitive skin, dab a little bit of lipstick onto your fingertips, then apply it to your cheeks and rub it in slightly. But don't try this for the first time immediately before going out."

When I was twelve, I decided that since my older sister was wearing makeup, I would, too. My mom lets us decide how we want to style our hair and do our makeup, so she didn't step in. For the next month I wore a ton of thick, dark foundation, and I used blush as a powder all over my face! People probably thought I was suffering from some kind of skin disease. Finally my aunt stepped in and showed me how to apply it.

—ORCHID2000

from: PRINCESS

Hey, I have a great beauty trick! A great way to cover up zits is to dab white eye shadow onto the zit, then putting your regular concealer over it. The white eye shadow will take away some of the redness. Be sure not to smear!

"*Actually, yellow counteracts redness better than white,*" says Leslie Blodgett, creator of Bare Escentuals. "*And be sure that the eye shadow doesn't have preservatives, waxes, and other ingredients that can clog a zit and make it last longer.*"

from: AMY

To make a big nose look smaller, dust a light brown shadow on the sides.

"*That's correct,*" says makeup artist Laura Geller. "*In addition, use a sponge (or felt tip) applicator to dust a light beige or off-white shadow down the center of your nose to call attention to the front and less to the sides.*"

About a year ago, I decided it would be a good trick to put lipstick on my eyelids. I was going for that red-eyelid model thing that was in all the magazines. I thought it looked really great, but about a week after I started doing it my best friend asked me if I had some kind of eye disease. I never tried that trick again!

—FIERCE

AUDREY DA COSTA

From Gwen's glitter to Marilyn's mondo makeup kit, veteran MTV makeup artist Audrey da Costa has seen it all. Here she spills her favorite star looks and even gives up some tips for us civilians.

Who makes the cut: THE FABULOUS FIVE

Shirley Manson: She's adventurous and changes her hair and makeup around in her videos, but she's still always tasteful. Shirley makes a statement with her makeup, but she doesn't actually need it at all.

Jennifer Love Hewitt: Love is cool. She's well put together: stylish but never overdone, and she keeps her fresh, teenage look. You can only look that fresh for so long, so why fight it? Girls like Brandy and Monica sometimes can look a little too done for their age with all that makeup and styling.

Gwen Stefani: Gwen is the first person I saw use rhinestones on her face in a really complementary way. When she came into the studio to promote "I'm Just a Girl," she walked in with her own makeup case—she's so used to having to do her own makeup from when her band didn't have a huge entourage, she just sat down and did her face herself, and I watched. She did very simple makeup—a white face and bold, purple lips and lined eyes. Then she got out all these different rhinestones and added just one or two in very flattering spots. The result was phenomenal. She was making a statement, but it was pretty, and it really worked.

Marilyn Manson: Marilyn travels with his own serious makeup kit, just like the one I have. Inside, he has a full stock of all these outrageous, watercolor-based face paints, and he applies them himself every time he makes an appearance. He'll start with very white skin, using a professional theatrical base called Aqua Color. Then he uses a very heavy dual finish product by M•A•C called Studio Fix over the white paint—that way you can't see his beard, and he gets a very flawless base like a canvas. Then he applies the watercolors.

Alanis Morissette: On the other extreme, Alanis has a no-makeup look, she uses her hair and cool clothes to make her statement. She's very no-fuss, very laid-back—a lot of women singer-songwriters are like that. And most of them, like Sarah McLachlan and Paula Cole, have such beautiful features and strong characters that they look great with little or no makeup.

You don't need a record deal to look like a million bucks. Just check out Audrey's no-nonsense beauty rules, and you'll always be ready for your close-up.

Know thyself: Makeup should always work to enhance your features. If all you want to do is make a statement, you can wear any old crazy lipstick. But to do it really well, find a lipstick that is like "wow" on you. One that complements your skin tone or goes with the clothes you're wearing. Otherwise people will look at your makeup instead of you. People should see the whole picture and not just say, "Oh, there's a pair of lips."

Erase the base: The most common mistake I see is girls using the wrong foundation. Even if you break out, you should still use a very sheer liquid makeup or just powder so people can see the freshness and youth of your skin. And seeing foundation lines is not cool.

Less is more: When they're still learning how to do their makeup, girls often just apply one thick line of eyeliner. But that can actually make your eyes look smaller. Go easy on the liner.

Read between the lines: Lip liner is essential because it helps lip gloss stay on. But the trick about using a liner is to use your finger and smudge it a little bit once you've applied it to your lips and before you put on gloss or lipstick. Otherwise you get that harsh, dark lip line that is really out of style (and it can make your lips look tiny).

Let you shine through: Overall, a positive self-image really outshines whatever you're wearing on your face. If you haven't been nourished to feel good about who you are as a person, then nothing that you do on the exterior will make a difference. It's difficult to be female nowadays. You're inundated with all these images telling you what the perfect look is, and it's very confusing. So the best thing is just to be yourself and have fun.

MOOD MAKEUP

WHY WEAR RED WHEN YOU FEEL BLUE?

According to New York–based emotional healer and success coach Aleta St. James, colors influence your moods in a major way, whether you believe it or not. Below, Aleta offers advice on how to use the emotional power of colors to your best advantage.

VIOLET Represents your mental abilities. Want to ace that big exam? Dust on some violet shadow or a smooth, translucent violet lip gloss. Oh yeah, it couldn't hurt to study, either.

YELLOW Represents self-expression. Dab a little on your lids and let your people know what you're really all about.

RED Represents empowerment. If you're feeling insecure, red nail polish will help you channel your inner diva.

ORANGE Represents sexual energy. A light dusting of orange gloss says hottie, not hoochie.

BLUE Represents focused energy. Paint your toenails blue and get people to give you way more than the time of day.

SCARLET Represents channeled intensity. So you're a little nervous about your speech—scarlet lipstick will ensure the show must go on.

PINK Combats rejection. Hot pink blush on the apples of your cheeks just might get your crush's attention.

MARY J. BLIGE

The platinum-selling singer talks about limelight, lipstick, and keeping it all real.

Your image has changed so much since you first came on the scene. You seem much more confident now. What changed, and how has this affected your self-image?

Well, I grew up. And I changed the people that I hung out with. And you know, you change the people, you change yourself.

Is it hard being in an industry in which you're judged so much by your looks?

Ugh. Yes. Sometimes I feel really sorry for myself and for other women. You have to stay the same ... or conform. Like, say if you're skinny when you start out, you've got to stay skinny. Like, you can't rest and stay home and gain an ounce of weight. 'Cause if you do, everyone's got something to say about it. It shouldn't be about that. It should be about the music, and people should like you for you, not how you look.

What are the top beauty tips you've picked up over the years from your mom, girlfriends, or the makeup artists you've worked with?

Lining my lips. It changes everything. And mixing two shades of lip color to make a better one. And learning how to do my eyebrows and make up my eyes. It makes a difference.

What do you do when you have to perform or do a public appearance and you don't feel like you look your best? Do you have any rituals or quick pick-me-up tips?

I say a little prayer. And you know, I say to myself, this is your job. Get out there and do your thing.

Who is your beauty icon?

I would say Chaka Khan. She was the ultimate and always looked so beautiful. Still does.

Do you have any advice for girls who are interested in getting into the music industry but are intimidated by having to fit into a certain beauty ideal?

Don't change nothing for nobody. You've got to be true to yourself.

POP IT, PLUCK IT, PAINT IT, BUFF IT

THE SKINNY ON YOUR SKIN AND NAILS . . .

You've sent in tons of ideas for making your skin the smoothest, your nails the neatest. Some of you are all about making goopy concoctions that get your skin clean and smellin' oh-so-yummy. Others have insisted that the best way to keep soft and smooth is to not wash your face, um, at all. One thing is for sure, you're well aware that your epidermises are showing, and you want them to look good. . . .

• SKIN CARE •

from: PENNY

My beauty tip/secret is that to keep my face nice and moisturized, I use mushed-up avocado as a paste, apply it to my entire face, and let it sit for ten minutes. It really works! I live in Washington, and it can get really dry during the winter. Well, while the effects of dryness are showing up on everyone else, they don't show on me and my buds.

"Avocado is fine for your face," says beauty expert Helen Lee. "The unsaturated fat content softens the skin. If you want to make an even better paste, get some glycerin at a pharmacy to mix in with the mushed-up avocado flesh. Glycerin, which should only be used on dry skin, helps draw moisture to your skin's surface."

from: BRETT

My solution for dry, flaky skin uses just one banana and a quarter cup of honey. First mash up the banana and stir it into the honey. Smother your clean face and neck with the mixture and leave it on for fifteen minutes. Add a little warm water and work the mixture over your face with your fingers, then rinse with cool water.

Sounds delicious, but this may not be the best thing for dry skin. "There's no data to support the idea that bananas are beneficial to your skin," says New York dermatologist David Bank. "And smearing a dry, flaky face with a thick layer of honey could block your pores."

from: CHRIS
Soak a washcloth in a bowl with equal parts milk and water. Then just tip back your head and lay the washcloth on your face for fifteen minutes. You'll get a clear, smooth, porcelain look!

"Milk soaks are normally recommended to have a soothing or anti-inflammatory effect rather than to make your skin smooth," says dermatologist David Bank. "They're a great 'medical' alternative to cortisone-based products for mild sunburns or if you have an allergic reaction to a makeup product. So, if you've got one of these conditions and you've also got milk, get it cold, straight from the fridge, and soak your face, using a clean washcloth, for just a few minutes at a time—even fifteen minutes is too long."

from: JUNIPER
Mix one part baby oil with one part body lotion and one part sunscreen. Then slide it on your legs. It looks great, and it's great for your skin. It also looks hot on your shoulders.

"Go for it. Baby oil, body lotion, and sunscreen are all great for your skin," says makeup artist Laura Geller.

from: JOANNE

Before I go to bed at night, I dab some alpha-hydroxy lotion on my lips. By the time I wake up my lips feel completely soft and supple.

"This will act as a mild exfoliator," *says Catherine Orentreich, M.D., a* *New York–based dermatologist,* *"which will make lips feel softer.* *But don't do it every night since it* *could be a little harsh. A dab of* *Vaseline is the best thing for soft* *lips and much less irritating."*

from: DMXGIRLS57

Here's my killer beauty tip that works: Don't touch your face, especially in affected areas. The dirt and oils from your hands transfer onto your face, leaving a gross residue that will cause more zits and breakouts.

"It's always a good idea not to touch your face," says Sheldon *Pinnell, professor of dermatology at Duke University Medical* *Center. "It makes a difference, but not because it prevents* *you from transferring dirt and grime. The big problem is trans-* *ferring oils from hand lotion. The most common skin problems* *are due to touching the face around the lips and chin with* *hands that are covered in hand cream."*

from: MICHELLE

If you're washing your face and you want to get a good, clean look with all of the residue off, the best thing to do is to rinse your face thirty or more times.

"Excessive washing of your face can be harmful," says dermatologist Pinnell. "There's no harm in using water repeatedly to rinse your face, but be careful you don't overdo it—this will dry out your skin."

from: CHILLY

A vitamin E pill punctured and squeezed into your moisturizer will make it as good as anything from any cosmetic line.

New York University dermatology professor Jerome Shupack isn't convinced. "I haven't seen any evidence that vitamin E offers a therapeutic benefit to the skin," he says.

from: SUSAN

Put baking soda in a warm bath instead of bubble bath. It makes your skin really soft and smooth.

"Yes, this is great," says Cheryl Renella, president and founder of Channings Day Spa in Chicago. "You can add one teaspoon of baking soda to your bath with two teaspoons of salt and three to four drops of

your favorite essential oil, like honeysuckle, vanilla, or lavender, to make it smell delicious, too." Dermatology professor
Jerome Shupack adds, "Baking soda will create an alkaline
solution in the bath, which tends to make the body release
dead skin cells. Salt will do the same thing. Make yourself a
solution that's as salty as seawater—then soak and emerge
with really soft smooth skin." Note: The baking soda can
change the pH balance of the water, so if you're prone to yeast
infections, this may not be for you.

from: TEDDY

Fine-grained sugar mixed
with bath gel is a great exfoliating scrub for your body.

"Once you put that on your wet skin,"
says dermatologist Diane Walder, "the
sugar will dissolve and won't do much

for you. Use oatmeal with the bath gel instead. This is a nice exfoliating yet gentle and soothing scrub."

from: HEIDI

To cure dry lips, massage with a soft toothbrush.

"If your lips are chapped, flaky, and sore, even a soft toothbrush will be too abrasive," says Gaudia Chevannes, spa director of the Aveda Concept Spa at Strawberry Hill in Jamaica. "What you'll need is something to soothe them, and good old Vaseline will do the trick perfectly and cheaply!"

BILLY B.

Makeup artist Billy B. has made up some of the most famous faces in the biz, including Lauryn Hill, Calista Flockhart, Rosie O'Donnell, TLC, and others. Here he talks about breakouts, brows, and avoiding the biggest beauty mistakes.

ROSIE

So Billy, what's the biggest beauty blunder that people make?

Almost 99 percent of the women that I see do their eyebrows wrong. Brows should have a gradual arch toward the outside corner of your eye, as opposed to the inside corner. Here's a fantastic trick:

1. Look straight in the mirror, take a pencil, and hold it straight to the side of your nose. Your eyebrow shouldn't extend past this point. It should start about where that pencil hits—straight above your nostril.

2. Hold the pencil next to your nostril, and rotate it across the pupil, so the pencil is slanted. Your arch should start where the pencil intersects your eyebrow.

3. Rotate the pencil even farther—to the end corner of your eye—and that's where your eyebrow should end.

What's the most important thing people need to know about beautifying themselves?

Good makeup starts with good skin. It's really important to do everything you can to educate yourself and learn how to take care of your skin. That's the bottom line.

So what's the best way to deal with zits?

Get into a regimen. Use a cleanser and a toner, exfoliate, and make sure you take your makeup off completely at night.

And think about what you do. If you're getting mysterious breakouts on your chin, it might be because you rest your chin on your hand all day. That stuff makes a difference. Also, drink lots of water (and stay away from soda as much as possible).

Serious acne, which is different from just occasional breakouts, can leave scars on your skin that you have to live with for the rest of your life. In these cases, you should see a dermatologist—it's well worth the money.

With so many skin-care products out there, choosing the right stuff can be totally confusing. How do you figure out what works without going nuts—or dropping serious cash?

Over-the-counter products that you can get at the drugstore are good, and they're getting better and better. Go and look at all the products, read the labels, and figure out what's best for your skin type.

Which beauty products do you consider the most important?

Everybody's makeup wardrobe is different. It depends on what you like. You could use just a coat of mascara (curl your lashes first) and some clear lip gloss. Or you could use a little brown eyeliner behind your top lashes, a coat of mascara, and lipstick. If you like blush, then add it to your makeup wardrobe.

Which of those trends are hot right now?

I love glitter. Like glitter eyeliners. I think they're fun and young and sparkly. I love all that. I love lip gloss. I love colored eye shadows and nail polishes.

What have you learned from all your fab celeb clients?

Be young while you can. I've learned that from Mariah, Missy, Lauryn—all of these women who started in show business at a very early age—they have always said that. You have your whole life to wear dark burgundy or red lipstick. Look young while you can.

·ZITS·

from: SUE
Okay, here's my tip. If you have zits, wash your face frequently and don't use too much soap or face wash that could clog your pores. Also, always make sure to drink lots and lots of water.

"When you get a zit, it's caused by an over-active sebaceous gland in the skin," says Darrell Rigel, M.D., president of the American Academy of Dermatology. "If you wash your face too often, you'll overstimulate these glands, and the drying effect will cause them to secrete even more oil. Just wash your face well twice a day, even a third time if you participate in any kind of sports. And do drink lots of water."

from: MINDY
Toothpaste gets rid of zits fast.

"My patients tell me the same thing," says NYU dermatology professor Jerome Shupack. "Toothpaste does contain drying and antiseptic ingredients, plus the consistency is perfect for a blob to stay on your face." FYI, if you have real problem acne and over-the-counter formulations aren't working, you should see a dermatologist.

from: GLITTERGIRL

I use dish-washing soap (the liquid kind) mixed with water to wash my face. Since it's made to take oil off pans, it will take oil off your skin. You don't want to use it every day, though, because you can severely dry out your skin.

"I vote against the dish-washing soap," says Dr. Darrell Rigel. "It's too strong and likely to irritate your skin and could leave it prone to infections and more breakouts. Johnson's baby shampoo is a milder cleanser, but only use it on your face if you have no face soap or face wash."

from: FOOGIRL

If you have lots of zits, then try this. After using your regular cleanser and rinsing with warm water, go over your face with an ice cube. Washing your face in warm water will open the pores, and going over your face with an ice cube will close the pores and keep oil and dirt from getting trapped.

"This won't prevent or clear up pimples," says dermatologist Catherine Orentreich, M.D. "But if you want to give yourself a home facial and mildly clean out blackheads, put your head over a bowl of hot water and cover with a towel. Follow with a face wash and finish with a cold water splash to close the pores temporarily.

from: LEELEE

Putting on Clearasil vanishing cream underneath your powder or foundation helps fight zits.

"There's no problem with covering up a pimple with either a medicated cover cream or makeup," says New York dermatologist Francesca Fusco, M.D. "What's really important is that you wash it off before you go to bed at night and that you choose a noncomedogenic product, which means it won't block the pores."

from: ANNIE

One of my friends told me that she wears a cute little sticker on a new zit, and after hours of wearing it, the zit starts to disappear. I guess it's because the stickiness sucks the zit away. If anyone asks you why you have a sticker on your face, just say, "Because I want to, silly."

"Impossible!" says dermatologist Francesca Fusco. "A sticker won't make a zit disappear. If anything, when a zit is blocked like this, you can actually make it worse by trapping oil in an open pore. The best thing to do is to use a medicated topical cover-up or over-the-counter acne medication that contains benzoyl peroxide or salicylic acid. When used as directed, these are very good."

from: ORANGECRUSH

Allergy drops take the redness out of zits.

> *"Most allergy medicines contain substances that constrict blood vessels to make the blood flow out of the capillaries and reduce redness," says NYU dermatology professor Jerome Shupack. "Therefore it would make sense that eyedrops or nose drops could lessen the redness of a zit."*

from: CATHY

My all-time favorite beauty tip is to put Listerine on zits to clear them up. It might sound crazy (and you might make fun of it—my friends tease me about having gingivitis on my face!), but it really works.

> *"Since Listerine has antiseptic qualities and the general belief is that a bacteria-free face reduces the occurrence of zits," says Professor Jerome Shupack, "this could be beneficial. In any case, it won't do you any harm."*

from: SNOWBOARD CHICK LAUREN

I never ever wash my face, and you know what? I've only had one zit in my whole life, and all my friends, who wash their faces religiously, have tons of zits. Hmmm . . . a connection, perhaps?

> *"Well, you happen to be lucky, but acne is due to many factors. And washing your face (preferably twice a day) will definitely*

reduce your chances of a breakout," says dermatologist Catherine Orentreich. "It's possible that you have fewer breakouts because you may not touch your face—touching can spread bacteria."

from: ELLEN

Hey, I have a wonderful secret.... I guess I can let you guys in on it. To get rid of zits and keep them away:

1. Get a bar of glycerin soap.

2. Get some sugar.

3. Wet the bar of soap and sprinkle the sugar onto the bar.

4. Rub the bar on your face ... cover every spot.

5. Be sure to scrub well or it won't exfoliate your skin.

6. Leave on for about five minutes.

7. Wash off, and voilà! Your skin is left baby soft, and soon those blemishes will disappear. It may not work on some skin types, but it works on me! I've been using it for six months, and I have no zits at all!

Dr. Sheldon Pinnell isn't convinced. "If you're using the sugar without much water, this is going to act as a very harsh scrub on your face. And if you add too much water, the sugar will dissolve. Plus if you have acne, this sandpaper action is going to *cause more inflammation to the skin and make any forming acne lesions actually rupture."*

from: MISSY

If you have bangs, hair spray them back into your ponytail. Oil from your hair can get on your forehead, causing zits when you work out.

It's true that oil from your bangs can cause you to break out, but dermatologist Catherine Orentreich warns, "Some people get acne on their foreheads from hair products dripping onto the face. If you spray back your bangs, there's a chance that when you sweat, the hair spray could run onto your forehead. A better solution is to wear a hair band or barrette to hold back your bangs."

from: SANDIE

Okay, I know everybody wants perfect clear skin, and I've found the solution. It doesn't matter what kind of skin cleanser you use just as long as you have some. Also, make sure to have some kind of moisturizer that you put on at night. Here are the simple steps to follow:

1. Wash your face in the morning and rinse with cool water. If you see pimples, put on a dab of benzoyl peroxide.

2. Wash with a cleanser at night and rinse with cool water.

3. Get some beauty sleep!

"Finding the right cleansing routine depends on the condition of your skin and your skin type—whether it's oily, dry, sensitive, or normal," says Annet King, training and development manager for the International Dermal Institute in Los Angeles, California. "You'll need to get the appropriate cleanser; typically one that's pH balanced." King suggests following this cleansing routine:

1. Apply a pea-size amount of cleanser (one that doesn't contain mineral oil) to damp or wet skin. Don't use too much or you'll dehydrate your skin.

2. Smooth the cleanser on your entire face and neck in circular motions going outward. Don't pull or rub too hard or you'll cause irritation. And don't use a washcloth unless it's fresh (a used one can be a haven for bacteria).

3. Rinse your face twice with warm (body temperature) water and blot dry.

4. Spritz with toner. Avoid harsh toners with alcohol, which can be too drying.

5. Apply a lightweight moisturizer with SPF (15 at least) to help trap moisture in your skin.

MATTHEW
VANLEEWEN

With stars like Jennifer Lopez and Drew Barrymore on his list of clients, makeup artist Matthew VanLeewen has more than a few beauty tricks up his sleeves. Here he lets us in on a few of the best. . . .

There are tons of amazing tricks you can do with makeup. But what are the basic rules to making up a great face?

If you're young, take advantage of this time because your skin will never look better. It's the best time to play with sparkles and shine, and there's no need to go crazy on foundation (maybe just a little powder).

When you're doing makeup, it's really important that you

create balance and harmony in the face. For example, if you have one eye that may be a little bit bigger than the other, work on learning how to open up the other one just a little. This rule really comes into play with lips. Most people have a bigger lower lip than an upper lip. I teach people to go easy on the lip liner on that lower lip and just add a tiny bit extra on the upper lip to create evenness.

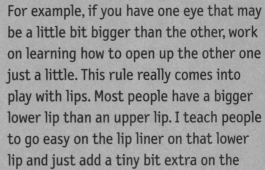

Also, don't feel like you have to build up every feature. Instead of focusing on your flaws, pick one thing that you love. In order for me to make someone look beautiful, I have to find what I love about their face. And there's something to love about every face. So that's what you should start with. You've just got to find that feature and play.

When you're going into glam mode on your clients, what part of the face do you like to concentrate on?

I'm a big fan of doing eyes first. If you're great at your eyes, you'll always be great at your makeup.

Eyebrows are really important because without any other makeup on the face, good brows can make you look really pretty. And bad brows can distract attention from your face. To really get your brows right, go to a salon or get someone you trust to at least clean up the stray hairs one time. You can then see what it looks like and do it yourself later, following that same line.

You do so many different looks for Jennifer Lopez—pop star diva, cover girl, serious actress. How do you do it?

There are days where I'll just start with a little color on her mouth and see where that takes me. And there are days where I'll do the eye makeup first. A lot of times with Jennifer, we go from rock star to street. We take just a little bit of moisturizer, wipe off her whole face, and just leave the eye makeup. It looks really clean, and her eyes stand out.

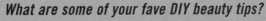

What are some of your fave DIY beauty tips?
Eggs as hair gel. Back in the 1980s when
everything was really punk, we used to use
a little tiny bit of egg white, and it would
make the best gel. Totally great for spikes.
So if you want spiky hair or if you want
the ends of your hair to separate,
egg whites are fabulous.

Yogurt is good for
dry, sensitive skin.
Oatmeal is also
incredible. If you mix
oatmeal and yogurt
together to create a lit-
tle hydrating mask and
leave it on your face for about ten
minutes, it's a wonderful skin softener.

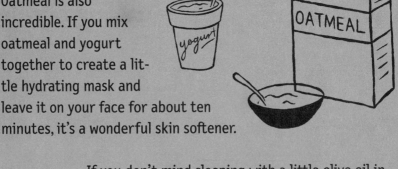

If you don't mind sleeping with a little olive oil in
your hair, it's an excellent conditioner. You can also
use it as a makeup remover. Just apply a little drop
to the face, then rinse—it's good for the skin, but
only if you don't have acne.

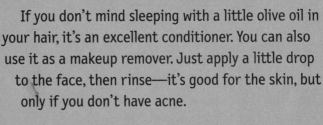

For dry lips use a scrub like Aapri or St. Ives
apricot scrub. It exfoliates and gets rid of the
dead skin.

I've actually used strawberries to make blush. Cut a strawberry in half, look in the mirror, and smile. Don't start in the front of the cheeks or the back—start in the middle (not at the roundest part of your cheeks, but maybe an inch back). Just pat the strawberry on that area a couple of times, and using your fingers, blend it out a little (not too much because you want to give it a second to stain). The color lasts all day. You can do this to your lips, too.

Okay, we're sure the celebs you work with never, ever get gnarly zits. But for mere mortals like us, zits are a regular thing. Any tips?

Tea tree oil makes a great alternative blemish treatment. Drew loves tea tree oil. She puts it in everything.

Witch hazel is a wonderful thing. It's a great toner, especially for acne-prone skin. It's also the perfect astringent because it doesn't strip the skin, but it does remove traces of oil and make the skin smoother.

What's the beauty rule that you swear by?

It's really important to clean the face—and take off makeup completely—before you go to sleep. With Jennifer, for example, I take off her makeup with baby wipes. If you don't have time or are too tired to go through the whole soap-and-water thing, at least use an astringent towel or an astringent-soaked cotton ball to get the product off your skin so that your face is clean and the pores are open.

·SHAVING/HAIR REMOVAL·

from: JEANIE

Instead of buying expensive shaving cream, use regular ol' hair conditioner. It works great and leaves your legs smelling very good!

"I don't see why this wouldn't work," says Debra Wattenberg, M.D., a New York–based dermatologist, "but you may be better off using a body wash because it's a soap with a moisturizer built in and will leave a smooth, slick finish. Remember, the actual closeness of the shave comes from the type of blade you use and the direction you shave in. Going against the growth of the hair will provide the closest shave you can get."

from: GINGER

I have a great beauty tip for anyone who tweezes their brows. Don't listen to people who say, "Put ice on your brows before tweezing." What that does is close the pores, making plucking more painful. Instead use a hot or warm cloth to open the pores, then pluck. You can put ice on afterward to soothe them!

"This is good advice," says Channings Day Spa's Cheryl Renella. "With open pores the hair will come out much less painfully. And a hot cloth prepares the skin perfectly."

from: GUMMIE BEAR

My best friend wanted me to pluck her eyebrows for her, but she flipped out and kept screaming ouch, so I got this idea. Before you pluck, put a little Oragel (that numbing gel for canker sores and stuff) over your eyebrows, and it will make it less painful.

"Great idea," says Ela Molczan, co-owner of Allure Day Spa and Hair Design in Manhattan. *"Anbesol will work great, too. Both products will numb your skin so you won't feel the pain. Plus you'll have some on hand the next time you get a canker sore!"*

from: RICKY

Do you get those annoying razor bumps on your legs after shaving? Well, take an astringent face wash and rub it onto the bumps. It may burn for a few seconds, but in an hour or so they'll be gone. Do this right after shaving so the astringent can start working right away.

"Unfortunately, astringents won't make any difference if you get razor bumps," says dermatologist *Francesca Fusco. "There are two kinds of bumps you can get from shaving. Sensitive little red bumps appear when you haven't properly wet the skin before shaving or if you haven't properly moisturized. For these kinds of bumps use over-the-counter hydrocortisone cream to take away the inflammation. The other kind of bumps are from ingrown hairs. These are hairs that were shaved off but have grown back into the skin. The best way to attack these is with exfoliators that contain alpha-hydroxy and beta-hydroxy acids."*

from: DMV

I heard that if you keep your razors in an inch or so of mineral oil (just enough to cover the blades), they'll stay sharp for a really long time.

"Ensuring that your blade stays sharp isn't a matter of what the razor is soaking in," says Vivian Orgell, beauty and stress expert and author. "It's a matter of which type of lotion you're using to shave with and whether you're using the proper shaving approach. But keeping your razor dry will prevent it from rusting or carrying bacteria."

I've always had a teensy bit of a mustache. Then one day my older sister said she'd show me how to bleach it so it wouldn't look so bad. So she sat me down and applied that cream bleach stuff and told me to leave it on until she said it was time to rinse off. Well, then she got a phone call from her boyfriend and totally forgot about me. I was sitting there practically crying because it stung so much. When she got off the phone, she came back in and screamed, "What are you doing? You should've taken that off ten minutes ago." My upper lip was so red and burned, my mom even let me stay home from school the next day.

—TAMMY

PAIN FOR VAIN

*Getting Hairless
Throughout History*

Today's hair removal processes are far from ouchless. But if you think ripping a strip of hot wax off your leg is horrifying, see how women before you have paid the price for beauty.

- In the Stone Age cave women used sharpened rocks and seashells to scrape away hair, the first example of primitive shaving.
- In ancient Egypt women applied hot wax and strips of gauze to their legs and ripped the wax away after it hardened, paving the way for the way women wax their legs today.
- Arabian women introduced bandandoz, a precursor to the epilator. They laced cotton string between their fingers to form a cat's cradle, then ran it briskly over their legs to simultaneously encircle and pull out the long hairs.
- American women in the early eighteenth century prepared caustic lye treatments, which they applied to their legs to burn away unwanted hair.

MISSY
ELLIOTT

Missy "Misdemeanor" Elliott talks about glamming up, dressing down, and getting in touch with her inner princess.

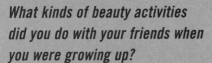

What kinds of beauty activities did you do with your friends when you were growing up?

I spent a lot of time with my cousins, and we would take one of those makeover dolls—you know, the ones with a head and shoulders but no body—and put blush and lipstick and whatever on her. And we used to play dress up all the time. We watched my mother and my aunt constantly dressing up, and we wanted to be so much like them.

Were you a glam little girl?

Actually, when I was really, really little, my mother used to put me in these lace dresses. And you know, I used to have lace socks and patent leather shoes. My mother always kept my hair in lots of bows. I think I spent so much of my childhood dressed up like that, by the time I was finally of age to make decisions about my clothes, I felt like, "Man, I just want to be comfortable." After the day I first put on a pair of sneakers, I started just wanting to wear comfortable shoes. And once I'd tried wearing jeans and jogging suits, you couldn't turn me back. Basically, just being in regular clothes is better for me.

What are your top beauty tips?

When I'm doing finger waves with my hair, I always use Nexxus gel. And for my nails, I never go past two weeks without getting them touched up.

What's the worst beauty blunder you ever made?

One time I made a mistake plucking my eyebrows. I was kinda young, and I had seen my cousins getting their eyebrows arched, so I took a razor and tried to do mine. I ended up taking off a whole eyebrow, so I had to take the other one off to make it match. Then I had to draw them on, and they were crooked. One looked like I was frowning, and the other looked like I was really happy. It probably took, like, three weeks for them to grow back. That was a long time to be walking around bald-faced.

So right now, what are the beauty products/tools you can't live without?

I gotta have eyeliner. I feel like I haven't gotten sleep in years without it. I also have to have lip liner. But basically, I don't wear much makeup.

lipliner

·NAILS·

from: NORDY

Here's a tip for the perfect paint job: Paint nails before a shower or bath and wait for them to dry. Once they're dry, the hot water softens the paint around the nail and rubs it off the skin where you went over the edges.

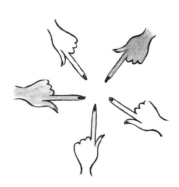

"You're probably better off washing your hands in the sink, where you'll have more control, or using a nail polish remover pen, which you can get from a beauty supply store. But if you want to try this, wait at least an hour for the polish to dry before taking a shower," says spa owner Lana Bargraser. "It's one thing if you're going to shower in cool water, but hot water may ruin the polish."

from: MAYPOLE

Sometimes in the winter my skin near the nail starts to peel off, so I put olive oil on that area to moisturize.

"I put almond oil on my nails to keep them from peeling," says Tina Bornstein, co-owner of Tony & Tina Vibrational Remedies. "It would figure that if almond oil works, then olive oil would, too."

from: FRANNY G.

When you paint your nails put on a white nail polish underneath your colored polish. You'll only need to put one coat of the colored polish, and it will be easier to remove because of the white polish underneath.

> *"If you put white under a dark color, you'll still need the second or third coats for the pigments to build up and give a good intensity of color," says Dineh Mohajer, creative director of Hard Candy Nails. "But painting white on underneath will give you a brighter color, and your nails might stain less." Note: White polish won't make your regular nail polish any easier to remove.*

from: ZOE CHIC

To make a sparkly polish, buy some shimmer powder and either mix it in with the polish or just brush it on your nails after you've painted them. Then put a coat of clear polish on top of that.

> *"Don't sprinkle the powder onto your nails while they're wet since you can't control how much you put on, and it can make them bubble up and spoil the finish," says Dineh Mohajer. "Adding some metallic or shimmer makeup powder to your nail polish pot is great. But be sure not to put too much in, or the polish will goop up and won't paint on right, and the excess will just fall to the bottom of the bottle."*

The Romans used sheep fat and blood for nail polish.

from: MARCY_MAMA
If I'm in a hurry and I have to paint my nails, I wait about a minute after finishing and then dip them in ice water to dry them faster.

Celebrity manicurist Deborah Lippmann says, "Ice-cold water is great for making your nails dry faster, but make sure the ice cubes are melted first so that they don't bump into your nails when they're still tacky."

from: TOSHI
When nail polish gets too thick, try adding alcohol to the bottle to thin out.

"My recommendation for getting the last bits of polish to flow out of the bottle is to roll it in your palms to warm it," says Jan Arnold, president of Creative Nail Solutions. "I wouldn't add alcohol, which could actually thicken what's left in there."

from: JENNY
Painting the tips of your nails white will make them look longer and neater.

If you bite your nails, this will just make them look torn and tattered. But if you have a substantial amount of nail," says Tony & Tina's Tina Bornstein, "then you're absolutely right— this can make them seem a tiny bit longer."

SHRED
BETTY

*The pro boarder
and Olympic bronze
medalist shares her
secrets for beauty on
and off the slopes.*

**As an athlete, especially
a snowboarder, what are
your specific beauty issues?**

Definitely the weather is a big issue. So I always try and
take care of my skin—especially my face. I do that by always
using a moisturizer with sunscreen. Even if it's cloudy, it protects my face. I use it even if I'm not snowboarding. If I'm
going to be out in the snow, I put on a waterproof sunscreen.
And I always wear Chap Stick and waterproof mascara. My daily
ritual is to put on my moisturizer, sunscreen, then mascara,
then I go snowboarding.

Did you like how you looked when you were younger?

I had braces my senior year of high school and my first year
of college, and I was a little old to have them. That was something I didn't like. But I guess you have to just accept yourself
as you are 'cause you can't really change too much. You just
work with what you have.

So did you ever try to do anything to take emphasis away from your braces?

It's impossible! I had clear braces, which are actually completely visible. I was really embarrassed in college because I was one of the only kids who had braces. But eventually I was just like, "I'll just look like a little kid for a few years, and then I'll have straight teeth." I just accepted it. That's kinda how I am with everything I don't like about myself. I just say, "Too bad." I have to live with it, and who cares, anyway.

What's your favorite feature?

My eyes. They're big and blue, and I don't have to wear glasses.

If you had to pull something out of your fridge to use as a beauty product, what would it be?

Probably avocado to moisturize my hair. My hair is dry since I'm always outside, and avocado is good for hair.

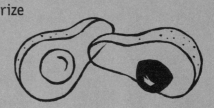

Who's influenced your look most?

My friends. I can relate to them. I can't relate to magazines and stuff because they're unrealistic.

When have you felt your most beautiful?

Just when I'm being myself. Your looks are very material. Beauty comes from the inside. That's what they always say, and it's true. If you have beauty within you, you're gonna be perceived as a beautiful person. Beauty isn't surface.

FEEL- GOOD BEAUTY

THE REAL SECRET TO LOOKING GOOD? HINT: IT'S NOT FINDING THE PERFECT LIPSTICK.

It almost goes without saying that all the makeup in the world, all the hair advice in the universe doesn't mean squat next to your inner beauty. (But of course you knew that.) And what's more, if you're not on top of keeping that inner you satisfied and fed and nourished, your outer beauty doesn't stand a chance of shining through. So here's a section devoted entirely to working on the you underneath the surface. And if you're wondering why it's the biggest section in this book, well . . . hello . . . it's the most important.

FOOD

Save yourself a trip to the makeup counter and get thee to the supermarket instead. The food you eat will determine how good you feel and whether or not you'll have good skin, hair, and nails. Here are some ideas for munching your way to beauty bliss. . . .

• Make sure to drink plenty of water to keep your skin properly hydrated. This is one of the best beauty tips for skin. Don't forget, you can easily get extra water by eating fresh fruit.

• "Eat fruits and veggies high in beta-carotene, like pumpkin, cantaloupe, carrots, and other yellow/orange fruits and veggies" says John B. Nowakowski, executive chef at the Regency House Spa in Hallandale, FL, "they're good for fighting acne."

• "If you have brittle nails," John adds, "try eating more canola oil or soy margarine. Also, be sure to get a sufficient dose of cauliflower, soybeans, peanuts, walnuts, and lentils, which are all rich in biotin and B vitamins and prevent nails from splitting and cracking."

• Cut back on junk food, animal fats, and heavy plant oils, like palm oil and coconut oil. You'll feel better (and this often clears up dandruff).

• Don't underestimate the power of protein in your diet for keeping your skin beautiful. "The combination

of protein and essential fatty acids creates strong cell membranes in the body, which promote healthy skin, hair, and nails," says Boston nutrition therapist Lisa Pearl, a registered dietitian.

• "Fish is a really great protein source," adds Lisa. If you're vegetarian, try to get as much protein as possible from nuts, soy, eggs, beans, and seeds to jack up the protein factor.

• "Snacking can be one of the healthiest things you do," says Lisa. "Everybody snacks, especially people who may not be able to get all the nutrients they need at every meal." If you're active in sports or if you skip meals because you get too busy, choose your snacks well, and you'll have no problem maintaining a healthy look.

• Take up to two tablespoons of flaxseed oil a day to help replenish oil lost from your skin and hair. It has a nutty, buttery taste, so you can sprinkle it on popcorn or eat it on baked potatoes.

Try these yummy snacks for a healthy body and a healthy look:

Trail mix: "Create your own personalized trail mix," says Lisa. "It's a great way to carry healthy food that won't spoil and is easy to eat. If you want more protein, add soy nuts; if you want extra fiber, add dried fruit. And for vitamins add some fortified breakfast cereal or sunflower seeds. Don't forget to spice it up with your favorite goodies, too, like pop-corn, pretzels, and a few M&M's or carob chips."

Simple snacks: Munch on baby carrots, celery, cucumber slices, pepper strips (green or red), rice cakes or popcorn, whole grain crackers, bread sticks, pretzels, low-fat granola bars, and pickles (pickles are high in sodium, so not too many of those).

Smoothies: Blend fruit juices with applesauce, pudding, honey, or yogurt. If you want, add ice to the blender for a cool smoothie.

Refreshers: Treat yourself to melon wedges, fruit salad, oranges, grapefruit, kiwi, pineapple, sorbet, sherbet, Italian ice, a frozen fruit Popsicle, frozen grapes, veggie juices like V8, and fruit juices (orange, apple, and berry).

Power snacks: These small meals, combining lots of carbohydrates and low-fat protein, have the nutrients to help you develop a healthy complexion, shiny hair, and flexible nails:

• Granola with low-fat yogurt and fruit slices

• Whole grain crackers with low-fat cheese and juice

• Pita bread with turkey, lettuce, and tomato and juice

• Whole grain cereal with low-fat milk and a banana

• Rice cakes with lowfat cheese and fruit slices.

WHO'S GOT THE JUICE?

Since they're jammed with vitamins and minerals and all that stuff, drinking fruit and vegetable juices will clear up your skin and put a sheen in your hair faster than you can save enough cash for the latest cremes and conditioners. So juice your own, or hit the health food store (to avoid the inevitable cleanup) and get ready to drink up.

Orange/grapefruit juice: These juices are high in vitamin C, calcium, and phosphorus. Mix them with carrots or beets, which are both necessary for good skin.

Cucumber juice: This is the original liquid rejuvenator designed to keep the skin radiant. It's a diuretic like prune juice and combats the effects of sodium and water retention. Pour a small glass and drink slowly.

Asparagus juice: Asparagus is a hearty vegetable that can help clear up zits and neutralize excess acids produced by eating spicy foods. Unless you have no sense of smell you'll want to hold your nose for this concoction.

Watermelon juice: The pH level of this juice is very similar to that of our human blood, so it's very easy for our systems to absorb and process it. Watermelon juice will flush the acid from your blood and lymphatic system, which will make you look and feel better.

Berry juice: Berries are a good source of vitamin C, plus they taste great and add fiber to your diet. So if you're thinking of skipping them, you might want to think again.

Carrot juice: Carrot juice contains all the good stuff needed for beautiful skin and hair, like zinc. Loaded with beta-carotene, it's an all-around healthy juice that helps clear zits and heal dry skin. And by the way, carrots really do help you see better in the dark.

STAR GRAZERS

Celebrities depend on looking beautiful for their careers. So to get the best advice on eating for beauty, why not look to the stars? Rich Guzman, owner of L.A. ROX—a fitness training facility in Los Angeles—and a certified nutritionist and personal trainer, fills us in on some food-related beauty secrets he's shared with stars like Selma Blair.

• Never be afraid of fats. Don't bother with fat-free food and diet sodas—it won't do you any good. Instead, make it a habit to drink at least two liters of water every day— and step up the amount of fruits and veggies you consume.

• Get a handle on acne by eating more leafy green veggies. They'll provide roughage to clean your system, flushing out the toxins that can create acne.

• Drink lots of juice—but not the kind with lots of preservatives or added sugar, which counteract the benefits that juices provide. Juice delivers nutrients to your body that it can't get from meats and fats.

• Eat several small meals a day. Keep them healthy and light—stay away from foods that are sugar laden or starch ridden.

• Skip chemical sweeteners altogether. If you want something sweet, try apple juice—it contains silicon, malic acid, and pectin, which make it great for the skin, hair, and nails.

• Make sure you're getting enough iron. Eat clams, dark leafy greens, and foods rich in vitamin C, like oranges, strawberries, broccoli, cauliflower, and pineapple —they're all excellent sources of iron.

• If you can stomach sushi, a little bit of raw protein is good for you. If you're not into that, try nuts and seeds, which also offer protein benefits.

·EXERCISE·

What you need for perfect skin and hair: plenty of water. Plenty of rest. Plenty of healthy food. And you guessed it, plenty of exercise. Read on . . .

Yep, exercise isn't just for jocks or people who want to lose weight. A good exercise program helps keep your hair shiny, your skin glowing, and your body strong. It's mad important.

See, to keep your skin clear, fresh, healthy, and looking really good, you gotta get your blood moving. You gotta get oxygen to those skin cells so they can repair themselves, replenish themselves, and keep themselves happy. Same goes for your hair and scalp. Oh, and nails, too.

And getting extra oxygen to your cells means breaking a sweat every now and then.

The good news? You can do it however you want. Snowboarding? Perfect. Basketball? Perfect. Dance? Perfect. Kick boxing? You get the idea.

And if exercise simply isn't your thing, try a few of these "nonexercise" exercises to speed up your heart rate and get your blood pumping:

• Speed walk instead of taking the bus.

• Rake the leaves, mow the lawn, vacuum—your parents will love you for it.

• Bust out your skates and cruise the neighborhood, midnineties style.

- Play Frisbee with your dog (borrow neighbor's dog if necessary).

- Actually participate in a game of tag with your little sister (borrow neighbor's little sister if necessary).

- Rediscover the joy of bombarding your friends with water balloons (or snowballs when applicable).

- Take up skinny-dipping. (Or take a swimming class at the local Y if that's too racy.)

- Use the stairs instead of taking the elevator.

- Wash the car.

- Ride your bike. Do tricks.

See, it's not which exercise you do that matters. All that matters is that you get moving, three to four times a week at least. For, say, a half hour or so. Still not sure where to start? Try yoga ...

I asked for karate lessons for my birthday last year. I go twice a week—and now I can kick my brother's butt.
—TANYA T.

YOGA

Yoga is an exercise centered around breathing. Its benefits include increased circulation, better posture, and a healthier complexion. Sounds good, right? But before you dive in, you've gotta learn the right breathing technique. So sit back and relax—we're about to get Zen.

"It's very easy to get into a habit of 'reverse breathing' or breathing wrong," says Michael Lechonczak, a senior yoga instructor at New York's Equinox Gym. "If you contract your stomach, chest, and ribs when you inhale instead of expanding them, you're breathing wrong. And when you don't breathe correctly, you actually tighten up all your muscles and your whole body becomes misaligned. Beautywise, this is the most counterproductive thing you can do! But if you breathe the right way, your whole body will receive oxygenated blood and you'll get that 'yoga glow.'"

How to Breathe for Beauty

Sit comfortably and close your eyes.

Relax the abdomen, rib cage, and chest in that order.

Inhale, letting your rib cage move slightly outward. Then exhale, drawing your navel back to the spine as you guide the breath out.

Continue to smoothly inhale and consciously exhale, allowing the breath to exit through the nose.

Observe each breath, but don't fight it or stress about whether you're doing it correctly or not.

Focus on making each breath fuller and deeper, but keep the breaths smooth and continuous. Continue for ten full breaths.

Notice by now that you're in a very different state of mind. It's amazing how breathing can affect how you feel, isn't it? Be sure to give your body permission to open and relax so you can truly reap the benefits.

Now, Here's a Simple Yoga Exercise

Stand up with your feet parallel and directly under your hips. Wiggle your toes and stretch side to side on the outer and inner edges of the feet.

Now contract your leg muscles and focus on mentally pushing your energy into the inner edges of your feet.

Pull in your butt so it's tucked slightly under your waist and bring your arms above your head (don't lock your elbows) with palms facing forward.

Arch your upper body back slightly and hold for two breaths.

Exhale as you allow your arms to float out and down. They should now hang at your sides with the palms facing forward.

Simply relax into this pose. It's called tadasana, or "mountain pose." There's no need to be rigid; just make the position work for you.

Now concentrate on your breathing again and breathe ten times in that slow, connected way. Observe how you felt before and how you feel after. There's no doubt that you'll look and feel more beautiful.

•BEAUTY SLEEP•

Ask any supermodel, and they'll tell you: Sleep is essential for looking good. The better you sleep, the better you look. It's that simple. So cuddle up with these tips for a sweet set of z's.

Skipped Sleep

If you've ever had a string of late nights, you know that sleep deprivation can leave you looking like yesterday's mashed potatoes—all soggy and lumpy and yicky (yes, yicky). Here's what's happening.

"The skin is the biggest organ in the body," says Cheryl Renella, owner of Channings Day Spa in Chicago. "If you're sleep deprived, your poor system will be too tired to pump blood around at the usual rate, and your skin will take on a grayish or sallow color. You might even feel cold, too, from lack of circulation. Your body won't have the energy to take a deep, reviving breath."

Breakouts are more likely when you're sleep deprived. Don't be surprised to see a bunch of blackheads and white-heads if you miss those z's. A tired body can't eliminate toxins the way it does normally, so impurities accumulate in the skin.

My junior prom was on a Friday night, and I had to pull an all-nighter on Thursday for this huge history paper I'd been putting off. The next day, I had huge circles under my eyes, so when I was getting ready that night I put on tons and tons of under-eye concealer. Little did I know that that would just make the circles worse! I ended up looking like a total zombie!

—HONEYB

Resting Easy

Now that you know how important it is to get yourself some shut-eye, here are a few pointers to achieving your prime rest rhythm:

Most important, listen to your body. You may need eight solid hours of rest while your pals need only six. To really look and feel your best, pay attention to how you feel after a good night's rest. If getting six or seven hours of sleep leaves you feeling like a two-toed sloth, try hitting the sack earlier.

If you aren't a good sleeper, don't get stressed. Take time to set the mood (Barry White style). Use moisturizing products at bedtime that contain lavender or chamomile (or create your own by adding these soothing herbs or essential oils to unscented products). A lot of people find it easier to sleep when there's some kind of background noise. Try listening to soothing music. If it's too distracting, try turning the volume down really low so that you can only hear the tune and not the words.

Afraid that you still won't be able to sleep? Take a warm bath before bed. Again, add a few drops of lavender oil to really unwind.

If you're too tense to sleep, get a friend to massage you. Not a boyfriend. That's something completely different.

Also, if you can't sleep because something is on your mind, try lying very still and taking several deep, slow breaths. This should help you relax. Try to wear loose pj's. 'Cause they're comfier, of course.

Always sleep with the room a little cooler than usual. You won't feel so dehydrated in the morning, and you'll be able to snuggle happily under warm covers.

If you've skipped a night of rest, don't sleep during the next day. It'll throw your body rhythm off, and you'll be hyper when you eventually hit the hay. See where this is going? Yep—a vicious cycle. If you must, take a catnap, but make sure it's no longer than twenty minutes.

ROCKET GIRL

The hot young actress from Third Rock from the Sun *and* 10 Things I Hate About You *dishes the dirt on photo shoots, phony looks, and her favorite lip gloss. . . .*

What was the first makeup item you ever used?

I used to ransack my mom's makeup drawer—I'd play around with weird nail polish, crazy dark blush, coral lipstick, and tacky blue eye shadow. The first time you watch how your face can transform with makeup is kind of cool.

What's your favorite beauty product?

I'm addicted to yummy-tasting lip gloss. If I don't have it on me all the time, I freak, and I always have it right by my bed when I fall asleep.

Who are your biggest beauty role models?

I think Patricia Arquette is the most gorgeous woman. There's something she exudes, I guess it's confidence, that's just awesome. I love the fact that she never changed her teeth to be perfectly straight—that's what makes her stand out and look different.

I also love Melissa auf der Maur and Gwyneth Paltrow. And Drew Barrymore has great style because she's just her—even when she was on the worst-dressed lists, I thought she looked hot.

What was your biggest beauty nightmare?

I look at pictures of myself two years ago, and I want to cringe because I looked so awful (especially my hair—a combination of long bangs and a fading dye job). But you know what? It's good to go through awkward phases like that because it makes you see how people treat you differently just based on your looks.

Do you have a surefire cure for zits?

I wish. Most of the time I have to wait until it goes away. Sometimes I use this stuff from Origins called Spot Remover, which makes your skin feel like it's on fire.

Do you have any home remedies for your skin or hair?

We have a lot of herbs in the yard at my house, so I'll put rosemary in boiling water and steam my face with that. It really makes me feel clean and gives me a healthy glow.

What's the biggest misconception about beauty?

Overall, how I look is something I'm so unsure of and insecure about, and I know other people feel that way, too, especially when they look at magazines and movies with so many perfectly beautiful people. So I want people to know that movie stars don't really look like that!!! They just don't. It's all an illusion created with lots of makeup and lighting.

When do you feel the most beautiful?

Not during photo shoots! It's nerve-racking to sit there with all these people focusing on how I look. I actually feel like I'm the prettiest when how I look is the last thing on my mind. Like when I'm just with my family having fun.

·CHILL OUT·

AROMATHERAPY

Aromatherapy is all about using certain smells (like the ones found in some essential oils) to influence your moods, whether you want to get pumped, get personal, or simply get chilled out.

We love the idea that smelling good can make you feel good, too. So we asked New York–based emotional healer and success coach Aleta St. James to line up some scents with the moods you want to muster. Sprinkle a few drops on a pillow, a handkerchief, your neck or wrist...and see what these scents do for you....

Jasmine

This is a chill-out scent. Dab some on when you're into kicking back with your buds.

Spearmint

Talk about the spirit of the new. This rejuvenating fragrance helps you leave all that emotional baggage behind.

Frankincense

Need to get focused? Sniff this age-old scent, and attack that project you've been putting off.

103

Chamomile

Check out this calming scent for a night of peace and quiet.

Patchouli

If you're short on willpower, patchouli will give you all the drive you need.

Lavender

Give your friends and family an early holiday gift—a bottle of lavender will pass on good calmness karma.

Neroli

Channel your innate fire and passion into something productive by wearing a splash of this scent.

Rose

Feeling insecure? Wear rose to regroup.

Sandalwood

Exam woes? Regain control with a sprinkle of sandalwood.

Ylang-ylang

Don't stand on the sidelines. Ylang-ylang can

help you make the kinds of decisions that will convince others you're a born leader.

MIX IT UP

Wanna get even more saucy with these scents? Try these creations:

Perfume

"The best way to create a personalized scent," says Tania Sethi at the Noelle Spa for Beauty and Wellness in Stamford, Connecticut, "is to combine one part rubbing alcohol with three parts distilled water and no more than five drops of three of your favorite oils. A great combo: ylang-ylang, lavender, and geranium. Put your exclusive, one-of-a-kind mixture into a plastic spritz bottle, shake, and get to it."

Shampoo

Try adding a few drops of these oils to baby shampoo:

If you want to feel **calm**: Add lavender oil.

If you want to feel **refreshed**: Add lemon verbena oil or peppermint oil.

If you want to **keep bugs away**: Add lemongrass oil.

If you need to **control dandruff**: Add tea tree oil.

If you need to **calm your irritated scalp**: Add rosemary oil.

Note: Don't go overboard adding the oils—you don't want your hair to look like a grease pit!

Lotion

Customize a generic body lotion like Lubriderm by adding

essential oils. For even more moisture, add a few drops of avoca-do oil. For extra healing benefits, add tea tree oil. If you're having trouble sleeping, add lavender oil and use before you go to bed.

I had a date with this guy I really liked. On the big night I took forever getting ready—you know, picking out a cute outfit, doing my hair and makeup, etc. And I must say, I looked pretty good. Just as I was dabbing on my perfume, my sister opened the bathroom door, causing me to spill a quarter of the bottle all over me. I reeked! The worst part was I didn't even have time to take another shower (I changed, but it didn't help much). His eyes were practically tearing up all night.

—PUFF

Conditioner

For extra moisture, pick up some macadamia oil at a gourmet food store and add it to your leave-in conditioner. To make just the ends of your hair softer, dab some oil on your palm, warm it in your hands by rubbing them together, then smooth it on the ends of your hair.

BUH-BYE, MR. BUBBLE

Beauty divas have enjoyed the pleasures of the bath throughout history. And if you're anything like us, you're no stranger to the luxuries of a dunk in the tub. So we asked Jenefer Palmer, owner of Natural Skin Care Products, to provide some completely different and DIY soak suggestions.

Tomato Soak

Okay, you're not going to believe this one. Fill the tub halfway. Then cut a dozen tomatoes in half and let them swish around in the water. Then get in and rub the tomatoes everywhere, even on your face. The tomatoes contain fruit acid, which will refresh your skin and leave it wonderfully smooth. Plus tomatoes are good for balancing out oily skin.

Old-School Suds

Epsom salts are the cheapest, yet the most reviving product you can get for the bath. Add a few drops of your favorite essential oil to a clump of Epsom salts. Then sit on the side of the tub while you're still dry and exfoliate your skin with the salts. When you're done, just slip in and soak.

Cleopatra Milk Bath

Do like Cleopatra and add milk to your tub for skin that feels like velvet. Get a quart of full-fat milk or mix up a pot of powdered milk and add to your tub. Stir well, then wallow to your heart's content while the lactic acid smooths your skin.

OUR FAVORITE INGREDIENTS

When it comes to DIY beauty, there's nothing better than stuff that's free—especially when it actually works. And we're not the only ones who think so. You've sent in tip after tip that uses supercheap, supercommon stuff you have lying around the house. Read on.

·CITRUS AID·

Juicy fruits aren't just good eats—they're also food for your face, and they contain all sorts of stuff that's good for your skin. But what makes them so versatile? Impress your friends with the info below....

What are radicals, and how can they hurt my skin?

Radicals are short-lived, highly reactive molecules found in the air. When they collide with other molecules oxidation occurs, which can cause cells to lose their structure and function.

109

What's C got to do with it?

Vitamin C molecules work as antioxidants because they stabilize radical molecules. For example, apples and avocados turn brown when exposed to the air (evidence of cellular oxidation), but dribbling on a little vitamin C in the form of lemon juice will slow this oxidation process down big time. At the risk of comparing you to an avocado (maybe you are like an avocado; we dunno), the same rules apply to the cells of your skin. So try these fruity beauty tricks:

LEMON FACE PEEL

Good for normal to oily skin, combine the juice and grated rind of one lemon, cover, and let stand for eight hours. Pat the mixture over your face, and leave it on until it starts to feel dry (no more than fifteen minutes). Remove gently with a damp washcloth, then rinse with cool water and apply your normal moisturizer.

LEMON SCRUBBER

Juice half a lemon, scoop out the pulp, and mix with two tablespoons of yogurt and enough cornmeal or oatmeal to make a thick paste. Then apply to your face, scrub, and rinse away dead skin cells.

LEMON NAIL WHITENER

Warm some olive oil in a saucepan over a low flame. Be sure to let the oil cool for at least three minutes, then dip your nails in it for five to ten minutes, massaging each nail really well. Once your nails have been throughly soaked push back the cuticles with an orange stick (from a drugstore), and shape them using a nail file. Then blot excess oil and rub with half a lemon to whiten.

GRAPEFRUIT HAIR SHINE

If you have colored hair, add some grapefruit juice to your regular shampoo. Smooth the mixture on your hair at the beginning of your shower, let sit until you're ready to get out, then rinse thoroughly. The grapefruit juice reduces the alkalinity left by color residue and smooths the hair shaft, giving your hair optimum shine.

PAPAYA-LEMON CUTICLE SOFTENER

Combine half a teaspoon of lemon juice with two tablespoons of fresh papaya or pineapple juice and two egg yolks, then soak your fingers in the mixture for thirty minutes.

from: PATTY

A really good way to bleach hair is to get a lemon and squeeze the juice onto your hair where you want streaks. Then go sit in direct sun (during summer) and wait while your hair gets streaked!

"You go, girl," says hair color expert Leslie Louise. "I like lemon juice to enhance blond highlights in the sun. You can use lemon on your hair every day at the beach, and it won't dry it out as long as you condition well afterward or combine the juice with conditioner on the beach." Since lemon juice only works to enhance your hair's natural highlights, it won't work for people with dark brown or black hair.

from: PLAYA_GIRL27

My trick to remove zits (I know this is going to sound phony, but all my friends and I are zit-free) is to wash your face and make sure that all the heads of the zits are popped. Then drench a couple of paper towels with lemon juice and completely cover your face. Let this sit for two to four minutes. Trust me, girls—it works. Then dust your face with powdered sugar and rinse.

"You really should try not to pop your own pimples," says Cynthia Gerardi, a dermatologist in private practice based in Westchester, New York, "because it's hard to do it right, and you can get infections and scarring afterward if you do it wrong. If you must pop them, make sure your face and hands are as clean as can be. Then allow yourself one squeeze per pimple. If this doesn't do the trick, stop here! Once you've squeezed, the best thing to do is cover the problem areas with zit cream. But beware, anytime you squeeze any type of pimple, you can still scar." Once you've popped the zit, you'll need to be careful about how you try to dry it out. "Lemon juice is a fruit acid, so it will have a drying effect," says Dr. Darrell Rigel. "However, avoid the powdered sugar because it could increase bacteria on your skin and lead to new breakouts."

from: HEATHER

Here's a good tip. Take half a grapefruit and some sugar. Dip the pulp side of the grapefruit in sugar so that the sugar sticks, then rub on rough skin. The acids in the grapefruit will soften the skin while the sugar sloughs it off to leave you feeling baby soft.

"This mixture is fine for exfoliation on places like the elbows and feet," says beauty expert Helen Lee. "But you'll get a better effect if you substitute lemon for grapefruit and salt for sugar! Lemons work better than grapefruits since they contain more acid and they bleach the skin well. Plus salt detoxifies by helping draw waste out of the skin. Just don't use this mixture on your face; it's way too harsh for that." And remember, sugar dissolves faster in water, so salt really is the way to go.

from: ROCKER_CHICK
Fade freckles with lemon juice.

"From a scientific point of view, lemon juice contains vitamin C and has bleaching properties, but I've never seen this method work on anyone," says dermatologist Francesca Fusco. "Freckles are caused by pigments in the skin, which are usually far deeper than any lemon juice could penetrate to work effectively."

•THE GOOP SCOOP•

You know it by its brand name, Vaseline, but technically this sticky stuff is called petroleum jelly or petrolatum. It's one of the cheapest and all-time-greatest beauty products. Tons of actresses and models swear by the stuff. Here's the scoop on the world's gooiest beauty gem. . . .

JELLY FACTOIDS

Petroleum jelly is composed of a mixture of oils and waxes and is noncomedogenic (translation: it doesn't clog pores). The waxes give petroleum its "firm body," and the oils help to keep it slick and spreadable so that it flows into the many surface cracks and crevices of the skin, forming a protective barrier that seals in moisture. Try the soothing solutions below with Vaseline or any other kind of petroleum jelly. Just one glob does the job....

SILKY PEDICURE

Rub petroleum jelly all over your feet at night and wear cotton socks while you sleep—it'll smooth out the rough spots.

HOT TUB HEALER

After being out in the freezing cold, a steaming hot tub

or soak in the bath feels like heaven. But guess what—nothing could be worse for your skin. Hot water will strip skin of its natural oils and leave it excessively dry, even itchy. But if you just can't resist diving in, take a shower first to get clean, then cover yourself in petroleum jelly and wait for twenty minutes for it to sink into your skin, then soak. It's a home-spa hydrotherapy treatment!

THE ROUGH TOUCH

Before going out into the cold, apply a light coat of petroleum jelly under your gloves to help retain your hands' natural moisture, prevent friction, and insulate your skin from frigid temps.

LIP SMACKER

The skin on your lips is thinner than on the rest of your body, and it can't remoisturize itself when you're out in the cold and wind for long periods. The end result is chapped and cracked lips—ouch! But this doesn't have to happen. Apply petroleum jelly every hour and add a little sunscreen for sunny days, snowy days, and when you're up in the mountains. Your lips will thank you.

from: ANGIE

All ya need is Vaseline! It's the best, baby! It's my favorite beauty product and it's the cheapest one out there. With Vaseline you can turn powdered eye shadow into liquid eye shadow with more staying power. Do I sound like a commercial yet? Put a little on your lips, and while you're at it, take a lipstick or some of your favorite eye shadow and blend with Vaseline to make a new shade of lipstick. It's very glossy, very nice. Put some on your cheeks for some shine, and voilà! A Vaseline masterpiece. So remember, pack eye shadow and Vaseline and let the magic happen.

> *Angie isn't the only Vaseline fan—mixing it with eye shadow is the most popular tip we received! "That's the beauty of Vaseline," says New York City makeup artist Maria Romano, "it's superversatile. However, stick to these guidelines: Don't use it everywhere, or you'll just end up looking oily. Choose just one place or two (cheeks and lips are a good combo); otherwise it's too overdone. If you do put Vaseline on your eyes, wear it only on your eyes, or you'll be overdoing it."*

from: CARA

If you're out of real lipstick, try this trick. You'll need a glob of Vaseline and a chunk of eye shadow. Mix the two together in a little jar, then apply! The bonus? You'll get tons of funky shades that you surely won't find in your local drugstore.

"Mixing your eye shadow with Vaseline to get lip color is fine, but make sure it's the right color," says makeup artist Sandy Linter at Z N.Y. "Stick to neutral tones, and stay away from yellows!"

from: QUINN

To make your own awesome fruity-flavored lip gloss, just mix some Kool-Aid and Vaseline together.

"I don't know if Kool-Aid would leave enough stain on your lips, but if you like the taste of it, then this sounds like fun," says makeup artist Maria Romano.

from: BRIT

Hey! Everyone says this is soooo disgusting, but it isn't. When taking off makeup, instead of using makeup remover, just use petroleum jelly. Just get a teaspoon-sized lump on your finger and rub it on your face. Leave on for a few seconds, and then get a piece of toilet paper and rub it off. Wash off any excess with warm water and soap.

Makeup artist Maria Romano agrees. "Petroleum jelly is a great tool," she says. "It's a cleanser and moisturizer in one. But be careful not to rub your face too hard to remove the makeup. And try using cotton balls or pads instead of toilet paper." Note: If you're super broken out or on acne medication, you probably shouldn't try this.

from: TABITHA

If you want to make your body shimmer, apply Vaseline, cornstarch, and blush or eye shadow.

"Why add the cornstarch?" says makeup artist Sandy Linter. "I would say crush your blush or eye shadow and pat it on your body where you want it. Then take some Vaseline and massage it on top to give your skin a shimmery effect."

from: DEBBIE

Here's one for girls with naturally great eyelashes who don't need mascara but would like control and shine: Put Vaseline on your finger and blink into it. Then comb through with an eyelash brush. Also, dab Vaseline onto the brow bone of your eyebrows. This will add extra shine and accentuate the shape of the brow. It will also help keep those thick problem brows in place.

"I love shine on the face," says makeup artist Maria Romano. "It's especially great for girls with dark lashes. A little petroleum jelly can make brows and lashes stand out a whole lot more. (Don't wear mascara, though, while wearing petroleum jelly, or it will smudge the makeup off very easily.) It's also a great brow groomer, and your brows will look really clean with it slicked over them."

from: GINGER

Vaseline, or my cheaper preference, generic petroleum jelly, can do more than just moisturize. If you don't have enough time to wait for your nails to dry, dab a bit of petroleum jelly onto each nail while the polish is half dry—it will act as a slippery barrier against dust and anything that may touch the nail's surface.

"Vaseline, baby oil, or any oil from your kitchen will do exactly this," says Aveda Concept Spa's Gaudia Chevannes. "It won't help your nails dry faster, but it will certainly stop dust from sticking to and smudging the nails. You can wipe it off after about two hours when the nail polish is finally set."

from: LAURA G.

My secret recipe for a feel-good lip booster: Fill a used lip gloss pot three-quarters of the way with Vaseline and the rest of the way with aloe vera gel, one drop of sunblock, and two drops of corn syrup. Then mix with a toothpick. For an extra tingle use peppermint oil (or peppermint liquid flavoring—it's the same thing).

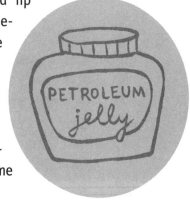

"This would give your lips a nice sheen and look glossy on your mouth, and the peppermint oil would be invigorating," says makeup artist Laura Geller.

·EGGS·

Okay, pretend they aren't food for a second. Eggs are actually oh-so-delicately-packaged beauty boosters. Fact is, eggs have been DIY beauty favorites forever, and even today they're recommended by beauty experts and addicts alike to condition, soothe, and soften. Here's the scoop.

The whites and the yolks of the egg contain protein, but the yolk contains all the fat. Both parts are commonly used for beauty recipes because eggs have the ability to bind ingredients and thicken mixtures. When eaten, the protein they provide benefits your skin, hair, fingernails, and toenails. And just one large egg is so complete, it gives you all the amino acids that your body can't make by itself. All this—plus vitamins A, D, E, and B, which are important for glowing skin and shiny, healthy hair. But remember, if you have acne or are using any form of medication, you should consult your dermatologist before trying any of these tips.

Yolk Shampoo

For a deep clean, combine two egg yolks, one cup warm water, and half a teaspoon of lemon juice or apple cider vinegar in a blender. Wet your hair with warm water and massage mixture thoroughly into your scalp. Cover your head with a shower cap (or if you don't have one, try tinfoil) and wait five to ten minutes. Remove cap and rinse thoroughly with warm water.

Veg Out

This trick will add moisture to your skin and give you a fresh, clean look. Combine one-fourth cup finely chopped cucumber, one egg white (already beaten), one tablespoon sour cream, and one teaspoon honey in a small mixing bowl. Stir until ingredients are mixed well. Smooth mixture on your face and neck and lie down for twenty minutes (destress and zone out to your fave meditation music). Rinse with lukewarm water.

Egg n' Lemon Shampoo

For a deep clean, combine 2 egg yolks, 1 cup warm water

and half a teaspoon of lemon juice in a blender. Wet your hair with warm water and massage mixture thoroughly into your scalp. Cover your head with a shower cap (if you don't have a shower cap, try using tinfoil) and wait 5 to 10 minutes. Remove cap and rinse with warm water.

Egg-on-Your-Body

For dry, flaky skin place one egg and one tablespoon lemon juice in a blender. Cover and blend until frothy, then turn blender to lowest setting, uncover, and slowly pour one cup safflower oil into mixture. Pour into a bowl or plastic container and apply to dry areas. Rub in well and leave on overnight.

Egg-on-Your-Face

Soothe your sensitive skin with this concoction. Combine one egg yolk, one teaspoon honey, one teaspoon corn, peanut, or olive oil, and four drops lemon juice in a small mixing bowl. Stir until mixture is a light paste. Apply to face and leave on for fifteen minutes. Rinse with lukewarm water.

Egg-Zit Treatment

To get rid of zits, mix one egg white, stiffly beaten, four ounces lemon juice, and three ounces orange juice in a small bowl. Apply to trouble spots and leave on for twenty minutes, then wash off with lukewarm water.

from: SHALOM

Use an egg white to shrink your pores and to help get rid of zits.

"Well, nothing shrinks pores permanently," says dermatologist Cynthia Gerardi. "But egg whites will do the trick temporarily since they're drying to the skin and will therefore help dry up acne pimples. Take caution not to do this too frequently, though— no more than once a week is fine. And if you've got dry skin, don't try it at all. Be sure you don't get any of the raw egg white in your mouth (in case it contains salmonella), and clean your hands and the kitchen counter thoroughly afterward."

from: BUBBLES

My face used to get really shiny all the time. Then my sister showed me this really funky skin treatment. Put a raw egg in a dish, mix it with a fork, and just smear it on your face. Then let it sit for about five to ten minutes and rinse it off. Your face will feel really soft and not greasy at all.

"With the yolk in the mix," says Dr. Gerardi, "your DIY face pack contains more fats and cholesterol, both of which are moisturizing. This recipe might be good to use on combination skin."

from: RACHEL

To get rid of oily, shiny skin, grab one egg and three teaspoons of oatmeal. Separate the egg and discard the yolk. Then use a whisk to beat the white until it's frothy. Add the oatmeal and stir until the mixture becomes a paste. Then apply to clean skin, leave for fifteen minutes, and rinse.

"If you work this mixture into the skin a little, it will exfoliate well," says Dr. Gerardi, "but you should try to put the oatmeal in the food processor first to break it up into really small pieces since large flakes could scratch your skin. Even so, do this routine no more than once a week."

THIS IS THE LAST THING WE'RE GONNA SAY

Okay, now you know all the tricks and tools you need to help look your best. Cool. And even though we know you know this, we're gonna say it, anyway:

Beauty is a powerful concept. It means different things to different people, and there are many ways to achieve it—a great haircut, a color that flatters your eyes, a healthy body exuding a healthy glow. But the real secret to true beauty? Being happy with yourself. Feeling satisfied with you. Finding that one thing you love—surfing, writing poetry, building kick-ass Web pages, whatever—and just doing it.

So why bother with the Kool-Aid lip gloss and avocado masks? Because when you look good, you feel even better. You're unstoppable.

But you knew that, right? We thought so.

Rock on,

Karen and Susan

FINAL WORDS

from: GIRLIE

I don't understand why everyone's always trying to look like a famous model or whatever. I want to look like me.

from: PHATTIE

Sometimes I don't take a shower or wear makeup or anything. Kinda like saying, "Who cares?" to the world.

from: INK.LIZARD

My hair keeps a natural shine because I never put chemicals on it. I also never wear makeup since a blemish isn't the end of the world and definitely nothing to stress over. Maybe I'm the only girl who finds "glamming up" a waste of time. Step away from the mirror and get to know the inner you.

from: LILWON

I like wearing makeup and I also like being a huge bum on the couch eating Doritos and I feel beautiful no matter what.

·ABOUT THE AUTHORS·

KAREN W. BRESSLER is a New York City-based free-lance writer who reports on fashion, beauty, health, fitness, and travel. She has written articles for many magazines, including *Vogue, Mademoiselle, Self, Seventeen, YM, Fitness, Elle,* and *Conde Nast Traveller,* as well as for international publications such as *Vogue Singapore, Australian Vogue,* and others. Her books include *Workout on the Go* (Andrews McMeel Publishing, Kansas City; 1998), *A Century of Lingerie* (Quarto Publishing, London; 1998), *Yogababy* (Broadway Books, New York; 2000) and several *Fodor's* travel guides. Since she covers the Caribbean regularly, Karen never leaves home without sunscreen and a really great aromatherapy moisturizer.

SUSAN REDSTONE is a British freelance writer who lives in New York City. When she's not straightening out her curly hair, she writes on fashion, fitness, beauty, travel, and lifestyle for international publications such as *Instyle, The New York Post, Time Out New York, Marie Claire, New Woman, Elle, Fitness, Shape, Woman's Own, Look, The London Evening Standard, The Sunday Times, Fashionwindows.com,* and more. Her favorite beauty splurge is new makeup but she spends hours playing D.I.Y. beauty spa at home.

beauty notes

Alima

hillry duff and all thows
peopl look relly nice.

hillory Duff and all
those people look relly nice
but they can de
to into there Lookes